Twin Cities Adventure Guide

2015

for families, visitors, and backyard adventure seekers

Twin Cities Adventure Guide

2015

for families, visitors, and backyard adventure seekers

First edition 2015

Turtle Town Press, Richfield, Minnesota 55423

Twin Cities Adventure Guide: 2015 for Families, Visitors, and Back Yard Adventure Seekers

Summary: *Twin Cities Adventure Guide: 2015 for Families, Visitors, and Backyard Adventure Seekers* is a comprehensive guidebook listing the many wonderful places to eat, learn, and have fun. The book features cross-references to discounted events and coupon sites to minimize spending.

ISBN-13: 978-1507871850
ISBN-10: 1507871856

Printed in the United States of America

This book was typeset in Calibri and Freestyle Script

Disclaimer: Listed organization, activities, and events are for the education and enjoyment of individuals and families in the Twin Cities metro area. Because information is gathered from a number of different sources including websites, emails, magazines, and organization printings; the accuracy of listed and linked information cannot be fully guaranteed. It is strongly suggested that readers double-check dates, times, and overall information before registering or attending listed events in case of change or inaccuracy of details. Postings of programs and events are not endorsements. You are strongly encouraged to seek as much information as possible by gathering feedback and references from trusted sources before you register yourself or your children for any of these activities to ensure their safety and enjoyment.

Contents

Introduction

The second year of *Twin Cities Adventures Guide* (formerly *Alphabet Adventures: Twin Cities Free & Frugal Family Fun*) brings you even more savings and exciting adventures to embark on with your family, out of town visitors, and for the local adventure seeker. In this guide you will find a comprehensive listing of all the great things the Twin Cities has to offer using a variety of sources including magazines, social media sites, and visitor guides.

Throughout the guide you'll find references to discounts including coupon books such as **Chinook Book and Chinook** mobile (*chinookbook.net*), **Entertainment** (*entertainment.com*), **Mall of America's** visitor guide that can be ordered (*tinyurl.com/24flvrr*) or found online (*tinyurl.com/p2qyqsx*). I have listed coupon numbers and expiration dates so you can find all the information you need in one place to easily plan your outings and save money while you're at it!

One of the best deals for both visitors and locals is **The Big Ticket Adventure Pass** (*tinyurl.com/mafezr2*), a 3-day pass that provides 30% savings on Mall of America and Twin Cities attractions including Nickelodeon Universe, Sea Life Aquarium, Water Park of America, Science Museum of Minnesota, Minnesota Zoo, and Great Clips Imax Theatre. AAA members can receive an additional 10% discount on *The Big Ticket* (*tinyurl.com/lvebz94*). Enter the code SUPER to receive an additional 20% off *The Big Ticket—bloomington-coupons.com/#bigticket*.

Members of organizations such as **AAA** (*tinyurl.com/kk5f6zo*), **AARP** (*tinyurl.com/qbw39z3*), **Minnesota Association of Community Theatres** (*mact.net*), **Minnesota Public Radio (MPR)** (*tinyurl.com/oejzb7p*), **Twin Cities Public Television (TPT)** (*tpt.org*) have access to numerous discounts. You'll find the majority of these memberships and coupon books quickly pay for themselves. AAA members can save $5 on the **Mall of America (MOA) Super Saver** coupon book. Print out the coupon on this website (*tinyurl.com/k7qmtr9*) and bring it to the Customer Service desk at the Mall to purchase this book. If you don't have AAA insurance you can utilize **Minnesota Northwest Convention & Visitor's Bureau** has a 50% discount for the MOA coupon book (*tinyurl.com/keu9g5e*). You can also find great coupons local here (*bloomington-coupons.com* and here *tinyurl.com/keu9g5e*).

Don't forget to check out daily deal websites such as **Amazon Local, Groupon, Living Social, Retailmenot, Yipit** for additional discounts. There's also discount online gift card sites that you can use to stack deals such as **Cardpool** and **Raise**.

My hope is that this guidebook helps families, visitors, and back-yard adventure-seekers to explore the Twin Cities and make enjoyable life-long memories that may even become annual traditions to build and maintain connections throughout the years.

Additional websites to check out for more Twin Cities family fun and savings: *exploreminnesota.com, familyfuntwincities.com, familytimesmagazine.com, hennepinchoosetoreuse.org, minnemamaadventures.com, mnparent.com, national.macaronikid.com, pocketyourdollars.com, thriftyminnesota.com, and kidapillar.com. tinyurl.com/lepngds.*

10% of all Twin Cities Fun Fun Guide 2015 sales benefit **Anaphylaxis and Food Allergy Association (AFAA) of Minnesot**a. AFAA is a 501(c)3 non-profit organization whose mission is to educate, advocate, and to support those with food allergies. Check out their website for more information: minnesotafoodallergy.org

> **Always check websites, Facebook, Twitter, and call ahead to ensure listed details are up to date and ask about additional discounts, memberships, and current events.**

With Best Regards,

Megan Meuli

tcadventureguide.com

AMUSEMENT PARKS

Above the Falls Sports
abovethefallssports.com
Minneapolis: 120 N 3rd Ave
612.825.8983

Canterbury Park Racetrack
canterburypark.com
Shakopee: 1100 Canterbury Rd
952.445.7223
bloomington-coupons.com 9/12/15

Como Town Amusement Park
comotown.com
St. Paul: 1301 Midway Pkwy
651.487.2121, parties
bloomington-coupons 9/30/15

Renaissance Festival
renaissancefest.com
Shakopee: 12364 Chestnut Blvd
651.487.2121, parties, AAA

Valleyfair
valleyfair.com
Shakopee: One Valleyfair Dr
952.445.7600

Wheel Fun Rentals
wheelfunrentals.com
Minnehaha Falls 612.729.2660
Lake Calhoun 612.923.5765
Lake Harriet 612.922.9226
Lake Nokomis 612.729.1127
Minnehaha Falls, 612.729.2660
Richfield, 612.861.9348
Lake Phalen, 651.776.0005
Parties, *Chinook* C388, 10/31/15
Entertainment D125, 126, H178
12/30/15, *Entertainment* mobile
& online

MINIATURE GOLF

Air Maxx Fun Center
airmaxxtrampolinepark.com
Eden Prairie: 7000 Washington Ave S
952.232.0096, parties, AAA

Big Bear Indoor Mini-Putt
yourgolfzone.com
Chaska: 825 Flying Cloud Dr
952.445.1500, parties
Entertainment D83, 10/31/15

Big Stone Mini Golf
bigstoneminigolf.com
Minnetrista: 7110 Cty Rd 110 W
952.472.9292

Bunker Indoor Golf Center
bunkerindoor.com
Minnetonka: 14900 Hwy 7
952.936.9595
Entertainment mobile& online

Centennial Lakes
tinyurl.com/9myy2cm
Edina: 7499 France Ave S
952.833.9580, parties

Eagle Lake Youth Golf Center
tinyurl.com/89yu2kw
Plymouth: 1100 Bass Lake Rd
763.694.7695, parties

Goony Golf of Spring Lake Park
goonygolfmn.com
Spring Lake Park: 1066 Cty Rd 10 NE
763.786.4994, parties
Entertainment D97, 12/30/15
Entertainment mobile& online

Grand Rounds
tinyurl.com/2c7dzry
Minneapolis: 1520 Johnson St NE
612.370.4937

Grand Slam—*grandslammn.com*
Burnsville: 12425 River Ridge Blvd
952.224.0413
grandslamcoonrapids.com
Coon Rapids: 2941 Coon Rapids Blvd
NW 763.427.1959, parties

Lilli Putt
lilliputtminigolf.com
Coon Rapids: 1349 Coon Rapids
Blvd, 763.755.1450, parties
Entertainment D59—60, 12/30/15

Maltees Ice Cream and Mini Golf
tinyurl.com/mffn2zd
Richfield: 6335 Portland Ave S
612.861.0668

Moose Mountain Adventure Golf
tinyurl.com/prgclkr
Bloomington: Mall of America
952.883.8809, parties, AAA
Entertainment D19 12/30/15
Entertainment mobile& online
MOA, 49, 12/30/15

Putt'er There
putterthere.com
St. Paul: 1300 Midway Pkwy
612.619.1800, parties

Saints North Maplewood
Family Skate Center
www.saintsnorth.com
Maplewood: 1818 Gervais Ct
651.770.3848, parties

The 10 Sports Centre
the10sportscentre.com
Long Lake: 2465 W Wayzata Blvd
952.417.6990, parties
Entertainment D74—76, 12/30/15
Entertainment mobile& online

Triple Play Sports
tripleplaysports.biz
Prior Lake: 5832 Industrial Ln SE
952.440.3330, parties

Arts and Crafts

American Girl
americangirl.com
Bloomington: Mall of America
877.247.5223, parties
MOA 188, 12/31/15

Amazing Threads
amazing-threads.com
Maple Grove: 11262 86th Ave N
763.391.7700
Chinook mobile 8/31/15

The Art Academy
theartacademy.net
St. Paul: 651 Snelling Ave S
651.699.1573, 5+ years, camps,
classes, teen programs
Chinook C222, 10/31/15
Chinook mobile 8/31/15, MPR, TPT

ArtiCulture
articulture.org
Minneapolis: 2613 E Franklin Ave
612.729.5151, classes, parties

Art Start
artstart.org
St. Paul: 1459 St. Clair Ave
651.698.2787, camps, classes,
events, parties, release days,
teen programs

Bead Monkey
thebeadmonkey.com
Minneapolis: 4959 Penn Ave S
952.929.4032, camps, classes
parties, *Chinook C262, 10/31/15*
Chinook mobile 8/31/15

BeARTrageous
artrageousadventures.com
Minneapolis: 2121 W 21st St
612.423.7554, camps, classes
parties

Bloomington Art Center
tinyurl.com/l36z22o
Bloomington: 1800 W Old
Shakopee Rd, 952.563.8575
camps, classes, parties

Build-a-Bear Workshop
buildabear.com
Bloomington: Mall of America
952.854.1164, parties
MOA 192, 12/31/15
bloomington-coupons.com

Cheers Pablo
cheerspablo.com
Burnsville: 13915 Aldrich Ave S
952.898.1901
Hudson, WI: 2421 Hanley Rd
715.531.8160
Woodbury: 8362 Tamarack Village
651.207.5034, classes, parties

Claymate Creations
claymatecreations.com
Minneapolis: Northrup King Bldg
1500 Jackson St NE #151
612.888.4252, classes, parties

Color Me Mine
colormemine.com
Eagan: 3324 Promenade Ave
651.454.4099
Maple Grove: 12155 Elm Creek
Blvd, 763.420.0005, camps
classes, parties

Crafty Planet—*craftyplanet.com*
Minneapolis: 2833 Johnson St NE
612.788.1180, classes, parties
Chinook C337, 10/31/15
Chinook mobile 8/31/15, MPR

Create Everyday
karimaxwell.com, classes
Minneapolis: 2605 2nd Ave S
Chinook mobile 8/31/2015

Darn.knit. {anyway}
darnknitanyway.com
Stillwater: 423 S Main St
651.342.1386, classes, parties
Chinook C338, 10/31/15
Chinook mobile 8/31/15

Digs Studio
shopdigs.com
Minneapolis: 3800 Grand Ave S
612.827.2500, classes, parties

Edina Art Center
edinaartcenter.com
Edina: 4701 W 64th St
952.903.5780 classes, camps,
parties

Heartfelt
heartfeltonline.com
Minneapolis: 4306 Upton Ave S
612.877.8090, camps, classes,
parties

Highpoint Center for Printmaking
highpointprintmaking.org
Minneapolis: 912 E Lake St
612.871.1326, classes, free events,
teen programs

Home Depot Kids Workshops
tinyurl.com/n7lgyd3 (20+ locations)

JoAnn Fabrics
joann.com/kidsstudio
10 locations, camps, classes, parties
Entertainment F63-64, 12/30/15

Kidcreate Studio
kidcreatestudio.com
Eden Prairie: 7918 Mitchell Rd
952.974.3438
Woodbury: 1785 Radio Dr, Ste F
651.735.0880, classes, parties

Kiddywampus
kiddywampus.com
Hopkins: 1023 Mainstreet
952.926.7871, camps classes
parties

Kidz Art
kidzartmn.com
Maple Grove: 7916 Main St
763.494.6957, after school camps
classes, parties, teens

Kidz Art
kidzartmn.com
Maple Grove: 7916 Main St
763.494.6957, after school camps
classes, parties, teens

Lakeshore
lakeshorelearning.com
Maplewood: 1721 Beam Ave, Ste A
651.777.0650
St. Louis Park: 5699 W 16th St
952.541.0991, events
Entertainment mobile& online

Linden Yarn & Textiles
lindenhillsyarn.com
Minneapolis: 5814 Excelsior Blvd
952.303.3895, 10+ years

The Linden Tree
thelindentreeshop.com
Minneapolis: 4404 Beard Ave S
612.961.7623, classes

The Loft Literary Center
loft.org
Minneapolis: 1011 Washington Ave
S, 612.215.2575, camps, classes

Manic Ceramic
manicceramicmn.com
Lakeville: 17685 Kenwood Tl
952.898.6978, parties

Maple Grove Arts Center
maplegroveartscenter.org
Maple Grove: 7916 Main St
763.250.1016, classes

Michaels Kids Club
michaels.com, 18 locations
camps, classes, parties

Material Girls Sewing
tinyurl.com/nrysvhd
952.201.3863, after school, camps,
parties, release days

Minnesota Center for Book Arts
mnbookarts.org
Minneapolis: 1011 Washington Ave
S, 612.215.2520, camps, classes

Minnetonka Center for the Arts
minnetonkaarts.org
Wayzata: 2240 N Shore Dr
952.473.7361 x16, camps, classes
memberships, parties

Mosaic on a Stick
mosaiconastick.com
St. Paul: 1564 Lafond Ave
651.645.6600, 8+ years, classes
parties

Northern Clay Center
tinyurl.com/km5puu8
Minneapolis: 2424 Franklin Ave E
612.339.8007, camps, classes
parties

Paint Your Plate
paintyourplate.webs.com
Edina: 5027 France Ave
612.929.6666
St. Paul: 1132 Grand Ave
651.225.8034, parties
Chinook C225, 10/31/15
Chinook mobile 8/31/15

Simply Jane
simplyjanestudio.com
Minneapolis: 5411 Nicollet Ave
612.354.3961, MPR, after school
camps classes, lessons, parties
release days, teens

Sewing Lounge
sewinglounge.com
St. Paul: 987 Selby Ave
651.645.7645, 5+ years
camps, classes, lessons, parties

Textile Center
textilecentermn.org
Minneapolis: 3000 University Ave SE
612.436.0464, camps, classes

3 Kittens Needle Arts
3kittensneedlearts.com
Mendota Heights: 750 Main St
651.457.4969, lessons 10+ years

Treadle Yard Goods
treadleyardgoods.com
St. Paul: 1338 Grand Ave
651.698.9690, classes 14+ years,
lessons 10+ years
Chinook C339, 10/31/15
Chinook mobile 8/31/15

The Yarnery
yarnery.com
St. Paul: 840 Grand Ave
651.222.5793, classes 8+ years
parties, *Chinook* C340, 10/31/15
Chinook mobile 8/31/15

Wet Paint
wetpaintart.com
St. Paul: 1684 Grand Ave
651.698.6431, classes

Minneapolis—*tinyurl.com/k7nvly5*

Cedar Point: 2100 Cedar Lake Pkwy
Cedar South: Cedar Lake Pkwy
East Cedar: 21st St W and Upton S
Lake Calhoun: 32nd Beach, 3200 E Calhoun Pkwy
Lake Calhoun N: 2710 W Lake St
Lake Calhoun: Thomas Ave S and W Calhoun Pkwy
Lake Harriet N: 4101 Lake Harriet Pkwy E
Lake Harriet SE: 4740 Lake Harriet Pkwy E
Lake Hiawatha: 4500 28th Ave S
Lake Nokomis: 5000 Nokomis Pkwy E
Lake Nokomis Main: 5001 Lake Nokomis Pkwy W
Theodore Wirth Lake: 3200 Glenwood Ave N

Anoka County—*tinyurl.com/n7s32mn*

Bunker Beach—*bunkerbeach.com*
Entertainment D73 exp 12/30/15
Coon Rapids: 701 County Pkwy A, 763.767.2895

Centerville Beach: 7401 Main St, Lino Lakes
Coon Lake: 5450 197th Ave NE, Columbus
Martin-Island Linwood: 22480 Martin Lake Road NW Linwood Township
Lake George Regional Park: 3100 217th Ave NW Oak Grove

Carver County—*www.co.carver.mn.us/parks*

Baylor—10775 Cty Rd 33, Norwood Young America
Lake Minnewashta: 6900 Hazeltine Blvd Chanhassen
Lake Waconia: 8170 Paradise Ln, Waconia

Dakota County—*www.co.dakota.mn.us/parks*

Lake Byllseby: 7650 Echo Pt Rd, Cannon Falls
Schulze Lake: 860 Cliff Rd, Eagan

Ramsey County—*co.ramsey.mn.us/parks*

Bald Eagle-Otter—*tinyurl.com/kog9n6a*
2015 N Van Dyke St, Maplewood 55109, 651.748.2500
Lake Gervais: 2520 Edgerton St, Little Canada
Lake Johanna: 3000 Lake Johanna Blvd, Arden Hills
Lake Josephine: Lexington & Josephine Rd, Roseville
Lake McCarrons: 1765 N Rice St, Roseville
Lake Owasso: 370 N Owasso Blvd, Shoreview

Long Lake: Old Hwy 8 and New Brighton
Lake Phalen: 1400 Phalen Drive, St. Paul
Snail Lake: 580 Snail Lake Blvd, Shoreview
Turtle Lake: 4979 Hodgson Rd, Shoreview
White Bear Lake: 5050 Lake Ave, White Bear Lake

Three Rivers—*threeriversparkdistrict.org*

Lake Independence: 2301 County Rd 19, Maple Plain
Bryant Lake: 6800 Rowland Rd, Eden Prairie
Cleary Lake: 18106 Texas Ave, Prior Lake
Fish Lake: 14900 Bass Lake Rd, Maple Grove
Medicine Lake, 12605 County Rd 9, Plymouth
Hyland Lake: 10145 Bush Lake Rd, Bloomington
Lake Minnetonka: 4610 County Rd 44, Minnetrista
Lake Rebecca: 9831 County Rd 50, Rockford

Washington County—*co.washington.mn.us*

Lake Elmo: 1515 Keats Ave, Lake Elmo
Square Lake: 5450 Square Lake Tl N, Stillwater
Afton: 6959 Peller Ave S, Hastings
Fort Snelling: 101 Snelling Lake Rd, St. Paul
William O'Brien: 16821 O'Brien Tl N, Marine on St Croix

BIKING

Explore Minnesota
tinyurl.com/pgme7xo

MN Dept of Transportation
tinyurl.com/pky8yun

National Park Service
tinyurl.com/nmaqcfw

Have Fun Biking
havefunbiking.com

Map My Ride—*mapmyride.com*

Metro Bike Trails
metrobiketrails.weebly.com

Pedal MN—*pedalmn.com*

Cyclopath—*cyclopath.org*

Trail Link—*traillink.com*

Anoka County
tinyurl.com/lxfxr76

TC Gateway
tinyurl.com/kep29sa

Carver County
tinyurl.com/3o7ax9m

Go Carver Go
gocarvergo.org/bike.php

Dakota County
tinyurl.com/p3pmuel

Hennepin County
tinyurl.com/mer7ueq

Met Council
tinyurl.com/mxh8n8u

Nice Ride—*niceridemn.org*

Ramsey County
tinyurl.com/lk6dxlr

Met Council—*tinyurl.com/mxh8n8u*

Nice Ride—*niceridemn.org*

Visit St. Paul
visitsaintpaul.com/bike

Scott County
tinyurl.com/n72t3zq

Washington County
tinyurl.com/kdp9e2p

HIKING

Explore Minnesota
tinyurl.com/posyo5y

National Park Service
tinyurl.com/kz3rel5

Anoka County
tinyurl.com/lxfxr76

Carver County
tinyurl.com/3o7ax9m

Dakota County
tinyurl.com/onoxdow

Lebanon Hills Regional Park
tinyurl.com/mermn73
Eagan: 860 Cliff Rd, 651.554.6530

Hennepin County
tinyurl.com/kxv23mu

Elm Creek Park Reserve
tinyurl.com/4ybypx8
Maple Grove: 12400 James Deane Pkwy, parties

Mill Ruins Park/Stone Arch Bridge
tinyurl.com/looh3tw
Minneapolis: 103 Portland Ave S

Mississippi River Walking Tour
tinyurl.com/ny9s2cy
St. Paul: 120 W Kellogg Blvd

Minnehaha Park Trails
tinyurl.com/pehv87q
Minneapolis: 4801 S Minnehaha Pk Dr

Water Power Park
tinyurl.com/ndrzu43
Minneapolis: 206 Main St SE

Winchell Trail
tinyurl.com/kz3rel5
Minneapolis: 3601 W River Pkwy

Ramsey County
tinyurl.com/lk6dxlr

Scott County
tinyurl.com/n72t3zq

Washington County
tinyurl.com/l46hlfo

Afton State Park
tinyurl.com/d2ztt
Hastings: 6959 Peller Ave S
651.436.5391

Photo courtesy Bob Mulcahy

BOOK STORES

Barnes & Noble
barnesandnoble.com
kids.barnesandnoble.com/kidsclub/
13 locations

Birchbark Books
birchbarkbooks.com
Minneapolis: 2115 W 21st St
612.374.4023

Buffalo Books & Coffee
tinyurl.com/lgs84nz
6 Division St E, 763.682.3147

Chestnut Street Books
chestnutstreetbooks.com
Stillwater: 223 E Chestnut St
651.430.9805, MPR

Common Good Books
commongoodbooks.com
St. Paul: 38 Snelling Ave
651.225.8989
Chinook C192, 10/31/15
Chinook Mobile 8/31/15
MPR, TPT

Creative Kidstuff
creativekidstuff.com
Edina: Galleria, 3555 69th St
952.926.4512
Maple Grove: 11647 Fountains Dr
763.424.2576
Minneapolis: 4313 Upton Ave S
612.927.0653
St. Louis Park: 665 W End Blvd
952.540.0022
St. Paul: 1074 Grand Ave
651.222.2472
Wayzata: 1135 E Wayzata Blvd
952.249.1707
parties, *Chinook* C264, 10/31/15
Chinook mobile 8/31/15

Dream Haven Books
dreamhavenbooks.com
Minneapolis: 2301 E 38th St
612.823.6161, MPR

Eat My Words
eatmywordsbooks.com
Minneapolis: 1228 2nd St NE
651.243.1756
Chinook C193 10/31/15
Chinook mobile 8/31/15

Excelsior Bay Books
excelsiorbaybooks.net
Excelsior: 36 Water St
952.401.0932, MPR

Half Price Books
hpb.com
Apple Valley: 7600 W 150th St
952.431.0749
Coon Rapids: 8601 Springbrook Dr
NW, 763.784.1500
Crystal: 5600 W Broadway
763.504.0262
Maplewood: 2982 White Bear Ave N
651.773.0631
Roseville: 2481 Fairview Ave N
651.631.2626
St. Louis Park: 5017 Excelsior Blvd
952.922.2414
St. Paul: 2041 Ford Pkwy
651.699.1391

Magers and Quinn Booksellers
magersandquinn.com
Minneapolis: 3308 Hennepin Ave S
612.822.4611
Chinook C196, 10/31/15
Chinook mobile 8/31/15, MPR

Micawber's Books
micawbers.blogspot.com
St. Paul: 2238 Carter Ave
651.646.5506
Chinook C196, 10/31/15
Chinook mobile 8/31/15

Moon Palace Books
moonpalacebooks.com
Minneapolis: 2820 East 33rd St
612.454.0455

A Novel Place
Osseo: 202 Cty Rd 81 Service Rd E
763.424.4122, MPR

The Red Balloon Bookshop
redballoonbookshop.com
St. Paul: 891 Grand Ave
651.224.8320, free events, story
time, *Chinook* C198 10/31/15
Chinook mobile 8/31/15

Sixth Chamber Used Books
sixthchamber.com
St. Paul: 1332 Grand Ave
651.690.9463
Chinook C199 exp 10/31/15
Chinook mobile 8/31/15, MPR

Subtext
subtextbooks.com
St. Paul: 165 Western Ave N
651.493.3871

Teeny Bee Boutique
teenybeeboutique.com
St. Paul: 1560 Selby Ave
612.644.2540
storytime, playtime
Chinook mobile 8/31/15

University of Minnesota Bookstores
bookstores.umn.edu
Minneapolis: 300 Washington Ave
SE, 612.625.6000, TPT

Valley Bookseller
valleybookseller.com
Stillwater: 217 Main St N
651.430.3385, MPR

Wild Rumpus
wildrumpusbooks.com
Minneapolis: 2720 W 43rd St
612.920.5005
Chinook C200, 10/31/15
Chinook mobile 8/31/15, MPR

AMF—*amf.com*
Little Canada: 61 W Little Canada Rd, 651.484.6501
Brooklyn Center: 6440 James Cir N 763.566.6250
Bloomington: 7941 Southtown Ctr 952.888.9248
Maplewood: 1955 English St 651.774.8787
parties, *Entertainment* D24, 12/30/15, *Entertainment* mobile & online

Apple Place Bowl
bogartsplace.com
Apple Valley: 14917 Garrett Ave 952.432.1515
parties

Blainbrook Entertainment Center
blainbrookbowl.com
Minneapolis: 12000 Central Ave NE, 763.755.8686
parties, *Entertainment* D91, 12/30/15, *Entertainment* mobile & online

Brunswick Zone XL
brunswickzonexl.com
Blaine: 1131 Ulysses St NE 763.561.2230
Brooklyn Park: 7545 Brooklyn Blvd 763.503.2695
Eden Prairie: 12200 Singletree Ln 952.941.0445
Lakeville: 11129 162nd St W 952.435.2695
parties

Classic Bowl—*classicbowlmn.com*
Coon Rapids: 11707 Round Lk Blvd 763.421.4402
parties

Country Club Lanes
countryclublanesmn.com
Excelsior: 5601 Manitou Rd 952.474.5959, parties, AAA
Entertainment D86, 12/30/15

Doyle's Bowling
doylesbowling.com
Crystal: 5000 W Broadway 763.537.8148, parties

Elsie's—*elsies.com*
Minneapolis: 729 Marshall St NE 612.378.9701, *Chinook* mobile 8/31/15

Ham Lake Lanes
hamlakelanes.com
Ham Lake: 16465 Hwy 65 NE 763.434.6010, parties
Entertainment D29, 12/30/15

Lariat Lanes
lariatlanes.com
Richfield: 6320 Penn Ave S 612.866.5311, parties
Entertainment D79, 12/30/15
Entertainment mobile & online

Louisville Lanes
louisvillelanes.com
Entertainment D71, 12/30/15
Shakopee: 3020 W 133rd St 952.445.8112, parties

Medina Lanes
medinaentertainment.com
Medina: 1500 Hwy 55 763.478.6661, parties
Entertainment D99, 12/30/15
Entertainment mobile & online

Memory Lanes
memorylanesmpls.com
Minneapolis: 2520 26th Ave S 612.721.6211, parties
Chinook mobile 8/31/15
Entertainment mobile & online

Midway Pro Bowl
midwayprobowl.com
St. Paul: 1556 University Ave 651.646.1396, parties
Entertainment D7, 12/30/15
Entertainment mobile & online

Park Grove Bowl
parkgrovebowl.com
St. Paul Park: 1020 Hastings Ave 651.459.4200, *Entertainment* mobile & online

Pinstripes—*pinstripes.com*
Edina: 3849 Gallagher Dr 952.835.6440, parties

PINZ—*pinz.com*
Oakdale: 7520 32nd St N 651.770.8000, parties

Sky Deck and Lanes
skydecklanes.com
Bloomington: Mall of America 952.500.8700, parties, MOA 56, 171, 12/31/15

Stars Strikes—*starsstrikes.com*
Wyoming: 5063 273rd St 651.462.6000, *Entertainment* D25 10/31/15

Sun Ray Lanes—*sunraylanes.com*
St. Paul: 2245 Hudson Rd 651.735.3222, parties

Super Bowl—*superbowlmn.com*
Ramsey: 6720 Riverdale Dr NW 763.421.7779

Texa-Tonka Lanes
texatonkalanes.com
St. Louis Park: 8200 Minnetonka Blvd 952.935.3427, parties
Entertainment D40, 12/3/15
Entertainment mobile & online

Town Hall Lanes
thlanes.com
Minneapolis: 5019 34th Ave S 612.767.3354

Tuttles
tuttlesbowling.com
Hopkins: 107 Shady Oak Rd 952.938.4090, parties
Chinook mobile 8/31/15

Afton State Park
tinyurl.com/d2ztt
Hastings: 6959 Peller Ave S
651.436.5391

Baker Campground
tinyurl.com/yjf4sog
Maple Plain: 2309 Baker Pk Rd
763.694.7662

Baylor Park
tinyurl.com/puhy3wx
Cologne: 11360 Hwy 212 W #2
952.466.5250

Bunker Hills Camp Grounds
tinyurl.com/oka7rux
Coon Rapids: CSAH 14 Main St
and Foley Blvd, 763.862.4970

**Cleary Lake Regional Park
Campground**
tinyurl.com/n7xbk4b
Prior Lake: 18106 Texas Ave
763.694.7777

Carver Park Reserve
tinyurl.com/3jj25ja
Victoria: 7025 Victoria Dr
763.694.7650

Dakotah Meadows
tinyurl.com/mccum37
Prior Lake: 2341 Park Pl
952.445.8800

Elm Creek Park Reserve
tinyurl.com/4ybypx8
Maple Grove: 12400 James
Deane Pkwy, 763.694.7894

Fish Lake Acres Campground
tinyurl.com/m48gwh9
Prior Lake: 3000 210th St E
952.492.3393

**Golden Acres RV Park
& Picnic Area**
tinyurl.com/nsha7xy
Stillwater: 15150 Square Lake Tr
651.4239.1147

Ham Lake Campground
tinyurl.com/lbp3lde
Ham Lake: 2400 Constance Blvd NE
763.434.5337

Hay Creek Valley Campground
haycreekvalley.com
Red Wing: 31655 Hwy 58 Blvd
651.388.3998

KOA
tinyurl.com/n39q474
Maple Grove: 10410 Brockton Ln N
800.562.6317
Jordan: 3315 166 St W 800.562.6317

Lake Elmo Park Reserve
tinyurl.com/kydozs4
Lake Elmo: 1515 Keats Ave N
651.430.8370

Lebanon Hills Regional Park
tinyurl.com/l4bjw2j
Apple Valley: 12100 Johnny Cake
Ridge Rd, 651.688.1376

**Rice Creek Chain of Lakes
Campground**
tinyurl.com/mrrw9p4
Lino Lakes: 7401 Main St
651.426.7564

St. Croix Bluffs Park
tinyurl.com/moypho5
Hastings: 10191 St Trail S
651.430.8240

St. Paul East RV Park
tinyurl.com/k77jalo
Woodbury: 568 Settlers Ridge Pkwy
651.436.6436

Shakopee Valley RV Park
shakopeerv.com
Shakopee:1245 Bluff Ave E
952.445.7313

Town and Country Campground
tinyurl.com/cdm7ppz
Savage: 12630 Boone Ave S
952.445.1756

William O'Brien State Park
tinyurl.com/ym7tm3
Marine-on-St. Croix: 16821 O'Brien Tr
N, 651.433.0500

Wildwood RV-Park and Campground
tinyurl.com/l5dxl5b
Taylors Falls: 37200 Wild Mountain Rd
651.465.6315, parties
wildmountain.com/vip-pass
V.I.P. pass with unlimited admission to
Wild Mountain—waterpark, Alpine
Slides & Go Karts, scenic boat tours, &
canoe & kayak trips

Check out the following websites for events and resources in your own backyard. Search the internet for community education, parks and recreation, community centers, visitor centers, and chambers of commerce. Look for Early Childhood Family Education (ECFE) and after school programs, athletic events, farmers markets (*stpaulfarmersmarket.com, mplsfarmersmarket.com, and tinyurl.com/pcw7ydz*), summer camps, movies and music in the park programs.

Anoka County—*www.co.anoka.mn.us*

Andover—*andovermn.gov*
Anoka—*ci.anoka.mn.us*
Blaine—*www.ci.blaine.mn.us*
Columbia Heights—*ci.columbia-heights.mn.us*
Circle Pines—*ci.circle-pines.mn.us*
Coon Rapids—*ci.coon-rapids.mn.us*
East Bethel—*ci.east-bethel.mn.us*
Fridley—*ci.fridley.mn.us*
Ham Lake—*ci.ham-lake.mn.us*
Lino Lakes—*www.ci.lino-lakes.mn.us*
Ramsey—*ci.ramsey.mn.us*
St. Francis—*stfrancismn.org*
Spring Lake Park—*slpmn.org*

Carver County—*www.co.carver.mn.us*

Chanhassen—*www.ci.chanhassen.mn.us*
Chaska—*chaskamn.com*
Victoria—*ci.victoria.mn.us*

Dakota County—*www.co.dakota.mn.us*

Apple Valley—*ci.apple-valley.mn.us*
Burnsville—*www.ci.burnsville.mn.us*
Eagan—*ci.eagan.mn.us*
Farmington—*ci.farmington.mn.us*
Hastings—*hastingsmn.org*
Inver Grove Heights—*ci.inver-grove-heights.mn.us*
Lakeville—*ci.lakeville.mn.us*
Lilydale—*lilydale.govoffice.com*
Mendota Heights—*mendota-heights.com*
Rosemount—*ci.rosemount.mn.us*
South St. Paul—*southstpaul.org*
West St. Paul—cityofwsp.org

Hennepin County—*hennepin.us*

Bloomington—*ci.bloomington.mn.us*
Brooklyn Center—*ci.brooklyn-center.mn.us*
Brooklyn Park—*brooklynpark.org*
Champlin—*ci.champlin.mn.us*
Corcoran—*ci.corcoran.mn.us*
Crystal—*ci.crystal.mn.us*
Deephaven—*cityofdeephaven.org*
Eden Prairie—*edenprairie.org*
Edina—*edinamn.gov*
Excelsior—*ci.excelsior.mn.us*
Golden Valley—*goldenvalleymn.gov*
Greenfield—*ci.greenfield.mn.us*
Hopkins—*hopkinsmn.com*
Independence—*independence.govoffice.com*
Long Lake—*longlakemn.gov*
Loretto—*ci.loretto.mn.us*
Maple Grove—*maplegrovemn.gov*
Medina—*medinamn.us*
Minneapolis—*ci.minneapolis.mn.us*
Minnetonka—*eminnetonka.com*
Minnestrista—*ci.minnetrista.mn.us*
Mound—*cityofmound.com*
Orono—*ci.orono.mn.us*
Plymouth—*plymouthmn.gov*
Richfield—*ci.richfield.mn.us*
Robbinsdale—*robbinsdalemn.com*
Rogers—*cityofrogers.org*
St. Anthony—*ci.saint-anthony.mn.us*
St. Bonifacius—*ci.st-bonifacius.mn.us*
St. Louis Park—*stlouispark.org*
Shorewood—*ci.shorewood.mn.us*
Spring Park—*ci.spring-park.mn.us*
Wayzata—*wayzata.org*

Counties and Cities

Ramsey County—*co.ramsey.mn.us*
Arden Hills—*cityofardenhills.org*
Falcon Heights—*falconheights.org*
Lauderdale—*ci.lauderdale.mn.us*
Little Canada—*ci.little-canada.mn.us*
Maplewood—*ci.maplewood.mn.us*
Mounds View—*ci.mounds-view.mn.us*
New Brighton—*ci.new-brighton.mn.us*
North Oaks—*cityofnorthoaks.com*
St. Paul—*stpaul.gov*
Roseville—*ci.roseville.mn.us*
Shoreview—*shoreviewmn.gov*
St. Anthony—*ci.saint-anthony.mn.us*
Vadnais Heights—*cityvadnaisheights.com*
White Bear Lake—*whitebearlake.org*

Scott County—*co.scott.mn.us*
Belle Plaine—*belleplainemn.com*
Jordan—*jordan.govoffice.com*
New Prague—*ci.new-prague.mn.us*
Prior Lake—*cityofpriorlake.com*
Savage—*cityofsavage.com*
Shakopee—*ci.shakopee.mn.us*

St. Croix River Valley—*saintcroixriver.com*
Hudson—*ci.hudson.wi.us*
Dresser—*villageofdresser.com*
Osceola—*vil.osceola.wi.us*
Prescott—*prescottwi.org*
River Falls—*rfcity.org*
Somerset—*vil.somerset.wi.us*
St. Croix Falls—*cityofstcroixfalls.com*

Sherburne County—*co.sherburne.mn.us*
Becker—*ci.becker.mn.us*
Big Lake—*biglakemn.org*
Clear Lake—*clearlakemn.govoffice2.com*
Elk River—*elkrivermn.gov*
Princeton—*princetonmn.org*
St. Cloud—*ci.stcloud.mn.us*
Zimmerman—*zimmerman.govoffice.com*

Washington County—*www.co.washington.mn.us*
Afton—*ci.afton.mn.us*
Cottage Grove—*cottage-grove.org*
Forest Lake—*ci.forest-lake.mn.us*
Hugo—*ci.hugo.mn.us*
Lake Elmo -*lakeelmo.org*
Lakeland—*lakelandmn.com*
Landfall—*cityoflandfall.com*
Mahtomedi—*ci.mahtomedi.mn.us*
Marine on St. Croix—*marine.govoffice.com*
Newport—*ci.newport.mn.us*
Oakdale—*ci.oakdale.mn.us*
St. Paul Park—*stpaulpark.govoffice.com*
Stillwater—*www.ci.stillwater.mn.us*
Woodbury—*ci.woodbury.mn.us*

Wright County—*www.co.wright.mn.us*
Albertville—*ci.albertville.mn.us*
Annandale—*andovermn.gov*
Buffalo—*www.ci.buffalo.mn.us*
Clearwater—*clearwatercity.com*
Cokato—*cokato.mn.us*
Dayton—*cityofdaytonmn.com*
Delano—*delano.mn.us*
Hanover—*hanovermn.org*
Howard Lake—*howard-lake.mn.us*
Maple Lake—*ci.maple-lake.mn.us*
Monticello—*ci.monticello.mn.us*
Montrose—*montrose-mn.com*
Otsego—*ci.otsego.mn.us*
Rockford—*cityofrockford.org*
South Haven—*south-haven.com*
St. Michael—*ci.st-michael.mn.us*
Waverly—*waverlymn.org*

Cultural Centers & Festivals

Canadian Days
tinyurl.com/42obemo
Little Canada

Danish American Fellowship
danebo.org
Minneapolis: 3030 W River Pkwy S
612.729.3800

Germanic-American Institute
gai-mn.org
St. Paul, 301 Summit Ave
651.222.7027

Hmong Cultural Center
hmongcc.org
St. Paul: 375 University Ave #204
651.917.9937

Irish Fair of Minnesota
tinyurl.com/mqjggnz
St. Paul

Japan America Society of Minnesota
mn-japan.org
Minneapolis: 43 Main St SE #EH-131
612.627.9357

Norway Day
sofn.com, Minneapolis

Polish Festival
tcpolishfestival.org
Minneapolis

Rondo Days Festival
rondoavenueinc.org
St. Paul

Swedish Heritage Day
svenskarnasdag.com
Minneapolis

Twin Cities American Indian Arts Festival
tinyurl.com/kszv7vv
Minneapolis

Galleries & Gardens

American Association of Woodturners Gallery
woodturner.org/gallery/
St. Paul: 222 Landmark Ctr
75 W 5th St, 651.484.9094

American Museum of Asmat Art
stthomas.edu/arthistory/asmat
St. Paul: 2115 Summit Ave
651.962.5560

Augsburg College Art Galleries
augsburg.edu/galleries
Minneapolis: 2211 Riverside Ave
612.330.1524

Banfill-Locke Center for the Arts
banfill-locke.org
Fridley: 6666 East River Rd
763.574.1850

Bethel University Galleries
bethel.edu/galleries
St. Paul: 3900 Bethel Dr
651.638.6400

Big Stone Mini Golf & Sculpture Garden
bigstoneminigolf.com
Minnetrista: 7110 Cty Rd 110 W
952.472.9292, parties
Entertainment D85 exp 10/31/15
Entertainment mobile & online

Caponi Art Park and Learning Center
caponiartpark.org
Eagan: 1220 Diffley Rd
651.454.9412
Tues Jun—Aug 10 AM free admission

Como Park's Marjorie McNeely Conservatory
comozooconservatory.org
St. Paul: 1225 Estabrook Dr
651.487.8201

Dowling Community Garden
dowlingcommunitygarden.org
Minneapolis: 46th Ave S & 39th St E
612.467.9545

Edina Art Center
edinaartcenter.com
Edina: 4701 W 64th St
952.903.5780

Franconia Sculpture Park
franconia.org
Franconia: 29836 St. Croix Tr
651.257.6668

Grand Hill Gallery
grandhillgallery.com
St. Paul: 333 Grand Ave, #101
651.227.4783, MPR

Greenberg and The Atrium Galleries
btacmn.org
Bloomington: 1800 W Old Shakopee Rd, 952.563.8575

Highpoint Center for Printmaking
highpointprintmaking.org
Minneapolis: 912 W Lake St
612.871.1326

Inside Out Gallery at the Interact Center
interactcenter.com
St. Paul: 1860 Minnehaha Ave W
651.209.3575

Japanese Gardens
tinyurl.com/msqljl3
Bloomington: 9700 France Ave S
952.358.8200

Landscape Arboretum
arboretum.umn.edu
Chaska: 3675 Arboretum Dr
952.443.1400, AAA, *Chinook* C188
10/31/15, *Chinook* mobile 8/31/15
Entertainment D44 exp 12/30/15
Entertainment mobile& online
12 and under free with adult entrance, Free Jan—March, Free 3rd Thurs Apr—Dec after 4:30 PM

Midway Contemporary Art
midwayart.org
Minneapolis: 527 2nd Ave SE
612.605.4504

Minneapolis College of Art & Design Gallery—tinyurl.com/qb83fwd
Minneapolis: 2501 Stevens Ave S
612.874.3700, camps

Minneapolis Institute of Arts
artsmia.org
Minneapolis: 2400 3rd Ave S
612.870.3000, 2nd Sun free family day

Minnesota Center for Book Arts
mnbookarts.org
Minneapolis: 1011 Washington Ave S
612.215.2520

Minnesota Center for Photography
mplsphotocenter.com
Minneapolis: 2400 N 2nd St
612.643.3511, classes

Minnesota Museum of American Art
mmaa.org
St. Paul: 1441 E 4th St, 651.797.2571

Minnetonka Center for the Arts
minnetonkaarts.org
Wayzata: 2240 N Shore Dr
952.473.7361, camps, classes, parties
Chinook C213, 10/31/15
Chinook mobile 8/31/15

The Museum of Russian Art
tmora.org
Minneapolis: 5500 Stevens Ave S
612.821.9045

Noerenberg Memorial Gardens
tinyurl.com/ptwdoyg
Wayzata: 2865 Northshore Dr
763.559.6700

Normandale Community College Gallery—tinyurl.com/lqm8jwc
Bloomington: 9700 France Ave S
952.487.8200

Northern Clay Center
tinyurl.com/lo5xjat
Minneapolis: 2424 E Franklin Ave
612.339.8007, camps

Northern Warehouse Artists' Cooperative
nwacartists.com
St. Paul: 308 Prince St
612.224.6360

Northrup King Building
northrupkingbuilding.com
Minneapolis: 1500 Jackson St NE
612.363.5612, 1st Thurs, 5—9 PM
Chinook C184, 10/31/15

Textile Center
textilecentermn.org
Minneapolis: 3000 University Ave SE
612.436.0464, camps, classes
Chinook C228, 10/31/15
Chinook mobile 8/31/15

Traffic Zone Center for Visual Arts
trafficzoneart.com
Minneapolis: 250 3rd Ave N
612.465.0233

University of Minnesota Art Galleries
sua.umn.edu/events/arts/
artsquarter.umn.edu
goldstein.design.umn.edu

Vision of Peace Sculpture
tinyurl.com/mju2nby
St. Paul: 15 West Kellogg Blvd

Walker Art Center
walkerart.org
Minneapolis: 1750 Hennepin Ave
612.375.7600, 1st Thurs night
1st free family Sat
Chinook C220, 10/31/15
Chinook mobile 8/31/15

Minneapolis Sculpture Garden

Minneapolis Gardens and Natural Areas
tinyurl.com/lsmwlvr
612.230.6400

Cowles Conservatory and Minneapolis Sculpture Garden
726 Vineland Pl
612.230.6400

Eloise Butler Wildflower Garden
1339 Theodore Wirth Pkwy
612.370.4903

JD Rivers' Children's Garden
2900 Glenwood Ave N
612.490.5095

Longfellow Gardens
3925 Minnehaha Pkwy E
612.230.6400

Loring Park Garden of Seasons
1382 Willow Street
612.230.6400

Lyndale Rose Garden

Lyndale Park Annual/Perennial, Peace (Rock) Hummingbird and Butterfly, and Rose Gardens
4124 Roseway Rd
612.230.6400

Minnehaha Falls Pergola Garden
4900 Minnehaha Ave S
612.230.6400

Nokomis Naturescape Gardens
E 50th St and E Nokomis Parkway
612.370.4900

Song of Hiawatha Garden
4801 S Minnehaha Park Dr
612.230.6400

Quaking Bog
1339 Theodore Wirth Pkwy
612.370.4903

Historical Attractions

Alexander Ramsey House
tinyurl.com/kubmq9m
St. Paul: 265 S Exchange St
651.296.8760, parties

American Swedish Institute
asimn.org
Minneapolis: 2600 Park Ave S
612.871.4907, camps, parties
Kids at the Castle, *Chinook* C218
311, 10/31/15, *Chinook* mobile
8/31/15, MPR

Anoka County History Center
ac-hs.org
Anoka: 2135 3rd Ave N
763.421.0600

Ard Godfrey House
tinyurl.com/ldp6cw9
Minneapolis: 28 University Ave
SE, 612.813.5300

**Bill & Bonnie Daniels
Firefighters Hall & Museum**
firehallmuseum.org
Minneapolis: 664 22nd Ave NE
612.623.3817, parties, TPT

Bloomington Historical Society
bloomingtonhistoricalsociety.org
Bloomington: 10200 Penn Ave S
952.881.4114

Boutwells Landing Museum
tinyurl.com/nfrfhsp
Oak Park Heights: 5600 Norwich
Pkwy 651.439.5956

Carver County Museum
carvercountyhistoricalsociety.org
Waconia: 555 W 1st St
952.442.4234

Cathedral of St. Paul
cathedralsaintpaul.org
St. Paul: 239 Selby Ave
651.228.1766

**Center for Holocaust
& Genocide Studies**
chgs.umn.edu
Minneapolis: 267 19th Ave S
612.624.9007

Children's Museum
mcm.org
St. Paul: 10 W 7th St
651.225.6000
camps, memberships, parties, AAA
bloomington-coupons.com
12/31/15, *Chinook* C178—180
10/31/15, *Chinook* mobile 8/31/15
TPT, free 3rd Sun

**Dakota City Heritage
Village & Museum**
dakotacity.org
Farmington: 4008 220th St W
651.460.8050, parties

The Depot Museum
whitebearhistory.org
White Bear Lake: 4th St & Hwy 61
651.407.5327

Edina Historical Center
edinahistoricalsociety
Edina: 4711 W 70th St
612.928.4577, parties

**Erickson Log House Museum
& Hay Lake School**
tinyurl.com/msrm63a
Scandia: 651.433.4014

The Fillebrown House
tinyurl.com/mr5tej2
White Bear Lake: 4735 Lake Ave
651.407.5327

Foshay Tower
foshaymuseum.com
Minneapolis: 821 Marquette Ave
612.215.3783

Gammelgarden Museum
gammelgardenmuseum.org
Scandia: 20880 Olinda Trail N
651.433.5033, parties

**Gibbs Museum of Pioneer
& Dakotah Life**
rchs.com/gbbsfm2.htm
Falcon Heights: 2097 W Larpenteur
Ave, 651.646.8629, camps
Entertainment mobile & online

Hennepin History Museum
hennepinhistory.org
Minneapolis: 2303 3rd Ave S
612.870.1329, MPR
Entertainment D98, 10/31/15
Entertainment mobile & online

Historic Fort Snelling
historicfortsnelling.org
St. Paul: 200 Tower Ave
612.726.1171, parties

Holz Farm
tinyurl.com/kmwaglj
Eagan: 4665 Manor Dr
651.675.5500

Indian Mounds Park
tinyurl.com/3z2p3of
St. Paul: 10 Mounds Blvd
651.632.5111

James Ford Bell Library
lib.umn.edu/bell
Minneapolis: 472 Wilson Library
309-19th Ave S
612.624.1528

James J. Hill House
tinyurl.com/nqacp2z
St. Paul: 240 Summit Ave
651.297.2555, storytime

The Landing
tinyurl.com/8923qw2
Shakopee: 2187 Hwy 101 E
763.694.7784

The Landmark Center
landmarkcenter.org
St. Paul: 75 W 5th St
651.292.3225

Lawshe Memorial Museum
tinyurl.com/kpwuvhh
So St. Paul: 130 3rd Ave N
651.552.7548

LeDuc Historic Estate
tinyurl.com/olly6a3
Hastings: 1629 Vermillion St
651.437.7055

Little Canada History Center
tinyurl.com/l27ewzm
Little Canada: 515 Little Canada Rd
E, 651.766.4044

Mill City Museum
millcitymuseum.org
Minneapolis: 704 2nd St
612.341.7582
Entertainment D80, 12/30/15
Entertainment mobile & online

**Minneapolis American
History Center**
maicnet.org
Minneapolis: 1530 E Franklin Ave
612.879.1700

Minnesota Governor's Residence
www.admin.state.mn.us/govres
St. Paul: 1006 Summit Ave
651.201.3464

Minnesota History Center
mnhs.org/historycenter
St. Paul: 345 Kellogg Blvd W
651.259.3000
Chinook mobile 8/31/15

Minnesota State Capitol
tinyurl.com/kbwj8wo
St. Paul: 75 Rev Dr. Martin Luther
King Jr. Blvd
651.296.2881

**Original Baseball Hall of
Fame Museum**
tinyurl.com/n7pj3lk
Minneapolis: 910 S 3rd St
612.375.9707

Pavek Museum of Broadcasting
pavekmuseum.org
St. Louis Park: 3515 Raleigh Ave
952.926.8198
Entertainment mobile & online

Prospect Park Water Tower
tinyurl.com/pq363zr
Minneapolis: 55 Malcolm Ave SE

Ramsey County Historical Society
rchs.com
St. Paul: 323 Landmark Center, 75
W 5th St, 651.222.0701, TPT

Richfield Historical Society
richfieldhistory.org
Richfield: 6901 Lyndale Ave S
612.798.6140

Robbinsdale Historical Society
robbinsdalehistoricalsociety.org
Robbinsdals: 4915 42nd Ave N
763.202.3529

St. Paul Police Historical Society
spphs.com
St. Paul: Office of the Chief
Inspections Unit, 367 Grove St
651.266.5573

**Scott County History Center
& Stans Museum**
scottcountyhistory.org
Shakopee: 235 S Fuller St
952.445.0378
Entertainment mobile & online

Schubert Club Museum
schubert.org/museum
St. Paul: 75 W 5th St
651.292.3267

Sibley House Historical Site
tinyurl.com/mos3nsc
Mendota Heights: 1357 Sibley
Memorial Hwy
651.452.1596, parties

The Stone Arch Bridge
tinyurl.com/6gbarl
Minneapolis: 125 Main St SE
651.230.6400

Wabasha Street Caves
wabashastreetcaves.com
St. Paul: 215 Wabasha St S
651.224.1191, parties

Warden's House Museum
tinyurl.com/pkvnfbp
Stillwater: 602 N Main St
651.439.5956

Wayzata Historical Museum
wayzatahistoricalsociety.org
Wayzata: 402 E Lake St
952.473.3631

Boulder Pointe Equestrian and Event Center
horseridingrocks.com
Anoka: 6612 189th Ln NW
612.716.9062, parties

Bunker Park Stable
bunkerparkstable.com
Andover: 550 Bunker Lk Blvd NW
763.757.9445, parties
tinyurl.com/oz2l69m, 12/31/15

HHH Ranch—*hhhranch.net*
Hastings: 16032 180th St E
651.338.2792

Pegasus Riding School
Pegasus-riding-school.com
Medina: 4550 Pioneer Tr
763.478.6472

Ridesport Stables
ridesportstables.com
Hamel: 22090 Strehler Rd
612.747.0621

River Valley Horse Ranch
rivervalleyhorseranch.com
Carver: 16480 Jonathan Carver
Pkwy, 952.361.3361

Rose Lawn Stables
roselawnstables.com
St. Francis: 24069 Rum River
Blvd, 763.753.5517, camps

Sunnyside Stables
sunnysidestables.org
Rosemount: 15400 Emery Ave E
651.226.2027, 6-13 years
camps, parties

Winterhaven Stables
Castle Rock: 507.581.4052

Ice Cream & Frozen Yogurt Parlors

Adele's Frozen Custard
adelescustard.com
Excelsior: 800 Excelsior Blvd
952.470.0035

Ben & Jerry's
benjerry.com/calhouncommons
612.378.9099
Minneapolis: 3070 Excelsior Blvd
Minneapolis: 702 Washington Ave
Chinook Mobile 8/31/15
Entertainment mobile & online

Bridgeman's Embers
bridgemans.com
Minneapolis: 4757 Hiawatha
612.721.6433, MPR

Cherry Berry
cherryberryyogurtbar.com
17 locations

Chilly Billy's
chillybillysfrozenyogurt.com
Minneapolis: 314 15th Ave SE
612.843.4278

Cold Stone Creamery
coldstonecreamery.com
Bloomington: Mall of America
952.851.0623
Eagan: 1264 Town Centre Dr, Bldg C
651.452.5700
Eden Prairie: 582 Prairie Ctr Dr, #250
952.943.9538
Hopkins: 768 Mainstreet
952.746.1970
Mendota Heights: 720 Main St #103
651.454.6001
Entertainment mobile & online

Cone Brothers Ice Cream and Candy
conebrothers.com
Richfield: 6633 Penn Ave S
612.455.0452
Entertainment C152, 12/30/15
Entertainment mobile & online

Conny's Creamy Cone
connyscreamycone.com
St. Paul: 1197 N Dale St
651.488.4150

Crema Café
cremacafeminneapolis.com
Minneapolis: 3403 Lyndale Ave S
612.824.3868, MPR

Dar's Double Scoop
darsdoublescoop.com
St. Paul: 1048 Rice St
651.489.2422

Edina Creamery
edinacreamery.com
Edina: 5055 France Ave S
612.920.2169

Freeziac
freeziac.com
Bloomington: Mall of America
952.303.6801
Eden Prairie: 16532 W 78th St
952.934.4748
Plymouth: 4105 Vinewood Ln N
763.383.0300
Maple Grove: 9408 Dunkirk Ln N
763.488.1599
Bursville: 1609 W Cty Rd 42
952.405.9727
Woodbury: 1960 Donagegal
651.348.2909

Froz Broz
frozbroz.com
Minneapolis: 3722 Chicago Ave S

Galaxy Drive-In
galaxy-drivein.com
St. Louis Park: 3712 Quebec Ave S
952.277.7777

General Scoop
Marine on St. Croix: 101 Judd St
651.433.2445

Grand Ol' Creamery
grandolecreamery.com
St. Paul, 750 Grand Ave
651.293.1655
Minneapolis: 4737 Cedar Ave S
612.722.2261

Hometown Creamery
FB HomeTown-Creamery
St. Paul: 2231 11th Ave E
651.779.4400
Entertainment C179, 12/30/15

Izzy's Ice Cream Café
izzysicecream.com, parties
St. Paul: 2034 Marshall Ave
651.603.1458
Minneapolis: 1100 S 2nd St
612.206.3356

Jackson's Coffee and Gelato
jacksonscoffeeandgelato.com
Minneapolis: 822 W Lake St
612.454.6613
Entertainment C180, 12/30/15

Lick's Unlimited
FB Licksunlimitedmn
Excelsior: 31 Water St
952.474.4791

Maltees Ice Cream and Mini Golf
tinyurl.com/mobvnl8
Richfield: 6335 Portland Ave S
612.861.9348

The Malt Shop
themaltshoprestaurant.com
Minneapolis: 809 W 50th St
612.824.1352

Menchies
menchies.com
St. Paul: 750 Cleveland Ave S
651.797.6428
Maple Grove: 8097 Wedgewood Ln
763.416.4656
Entertainment mobile & online

Ice Cream & Frozen Yogurt Parlors

Neighborhood Ice Cream Shoppe
FB NeighborhoodIceCreamShoppe
Edina: 6137 Kellogg Ave
952.922.9597

Nelson's Ice Cream
nelsonsicecream.biz
St. Paul: 454 Snelling Ave S
651.348.8990
Stillwater: 920 Olive St W
651.430.1103

Peppermint Twist Drive-In
thepepperminttwist.com
Delano: 181 Babcock Blvd W
763.972.2575

Pumphouse Creamery
pumphouse-creamery.com
Minneapolis: 4754 Chicago Ave S
612.825.2021

Scoops Ice Cream and More
ilovescoopsmn.com
Bloomington: 7700 W Old
Shakopee Rd, 612.849.3909
ilovescoopsmn.com/coupons

Selma's Ice Cream Parlour
selmasparlour.com
Afton: 3419 St. Croix Tr S
651.436.5131

Sub Zero Ice Cream and Yogurt
subzeroicecream.com
Chanhassen: 7828 Market Blvd
Eden Prairie: 8251 Flying Cloud Dr
Entertainment mobile & online

Sebastian Joe's
sebastianjoesicecream.com
Minneapolis: 1007 Franklin Ave S
612.870.0065
Minneapolis: 4321 Upton Ave S
612.926.7916
Chinook Mobile8/31/15

Sonny's Ice Cream
sonnysicecream.com
Minneapolis: 3403 Lyndale Ave S
612.824.3868
Chinook mobile 8/31/15

Snuffy's Malt Shop
snuffysmaltshops.com
snuffysroseville.com
Edina: 4502 Valley View Rd
952.920.0949
St. Paul: 244 Cleveland Ave S
651.690.1843
Minnetonka: 17519 Minnetonka
Blvd 952.475.1850
St. Paul: 1125 Larpenteur Ave W
651.488.0241
Entertainment mobile & online
tinyurl.com/qh8a9gw

Tutti Frutti
tfyogurt.com
Maple Grove: 7781 Main St
Entertainment mobile & online

Sweet Science Ice Cream
sweetscienceicecream.com
St. Paul: 285 George St
651.300.9333

TCBY
tcby.com
Albertville: 6415 Lebeaux Ave N
#C80
Burnsville: 1042 Burnsville Ctr 1042
Minneapolis: 600 Hennepin Ave #260
Roseville: 120 Rosedale Ctr
Entertainment Mobileand Online

Two Scoops Ice Cream Shoppe
twoscoopsmn.com
Anoka: 1918 2nd Ave S
763.323.0622

(yo) gurt [lab]
yogurtlabs.com
Apple Valley: 7394 W 153rd St #103
952.683.1599
Edina: 5007 France Ave S
612.315.3651
Eagan: 2000 Rahncliff Ct #200
651.493.2167
Hopkins: 525 Blake Rd #108
952.417.6168
Maple Grove: 7781 Main St N
763.205.1687
Minneapolis:2935 Girard Ave
612.353.4209
Minneapolis: 309 SE Oak St
612.331.3978
Minneapolis: 3100 Excelsior Blvd
612.926.8212
Minneapolis: 80 8th St S #226
612.886.3084
Onalaska: 1230 Crossing Meadows Dr
608.519.5939
Wayzata: 701 E Lake St, #150
952.300.8676
Woodbury: 610 Woodbury Dr, #200
651.528.6522

A.C.E.S. Flight Simulation Center
flyaces.com
Bloomington: Mall of America
952.920.3519
parties, MOA 47 12/31/15

Action Packed Paintball
actionpackedpaintball.com
Jordan: 8200 Old Hwy 169
952.492.6776, parties
Entertainment D88, 10/31/15
Entertainment mobile & online

Adventure Peak in Edinborough Park
edinboroughpark.com
Edina: 7700 York Ave S
952.833.9540, parties

Air Maxx Trampoline Park and Fun Center
airmaxxtrampolinepark.com
Eden Prairie: 7000 Washington
Ave S, 952.232.0096, parties
AAA, *Entertainment* D30-31
12/30/15, *Entertainment* mobile
& online

Amazing Mirror Maze
mirrormazes.com
Bloomington: Mall of America
952.854.5345, MOA 48, 12/31/15

Big Thrill Factory
bigthrillfactory.com
Minnetonka: 17585 Hwy 7
952.698.7700, parties, AAA
Entertainment D20—22 12/30/15
Entertainment mobile & online

Blainbrook Entertainment Center
blainbrookbowl.com
Minneapolis: 12000 Central Ave
NE 763.755.8686

The Blast Indoor Playground
eagancommunitycenter.com
Eagan: 1501 Central Pkwy
651.675.5550, parties

Brick Mania
brickmania.com
Minneapolis: 1620 Central Ave NE
#170, 612.545.5263

Brooklyn Center Community Center
tinyurl.com/l2as8on
Minneapolis: 6301 Shingle Creek
Pkwy, 763.569.3400, parties
Entertainment mobile & online

Brown Family Adventure
adventureparkmn.com
Ham Lake: 14200 Lincoln St NE
763.331.0265, parties

Brunswick Zone XL
bowlbrunswick.com
Lakeville: 162nd St W
952.435.2695, parties

Chuck-E-Cheese's
chuckecheese.com
Blaine: 8943 University Ave NE
763.785.2966
Burnsville: 1025 Burnsville Center
952.892.7786
Edina: 7505 France Ave S
952.831.4077
Maple Grove: 12945 Elm Creek Blvd
763.494.5520
West St. Paul: 1422 S Roberts
651.453.1066
Woodbury: 445 Commerce Dr
651.702.0700, parties

Creative Lounge
FB Creative Lounge
Bloomington: 9424 Lyndale Ave S
952.210.5119, parties

Dave and Buster's
daveandbusters.com, parties
Maple Grove: 11780 Fountains Wy
763.493.9815

Eagles Nest
tinyurl.com/cjw6sht
New Brighton: 400 10th St NW
651.638.2130, parties
Entertainment D51, 12/30/15
Entertainment mobile & online

Gamin Ride And Glamour Ride
gaminride.com
612.460.5001, parties

Gigi's Playhouse
gigisplayhouse.org/twincities/
St. Louis Park: 4740 Park Glen Rd
952.926.3660
Down Syndrome play and resources

Good Times Park
goodtimespark.com
Eagan: 3625 Northwood Circle #100
651.454.5736, parties

Grand Slam
grandslammn.com
Burnsville: 12425 River Ridge Blvd
952.224.0413
Coon Rapids: 2941 Coon Rapids Blvd
NW 763.427.1959, parties

Inspiration Performing Arts Center
www.inspiration-dance.com
Mahtomedia: 758 Stillwater Rd
651.241.8713, parties

Ikea Småland
tinyurl.com/92etnow
Chinook C-384, 10/31/14
Bloomington: 8000 IKEA Way
888.888.4532

Lego Imagination Center
tinyurl.com/lzgomjk
MOA 217, 12/31/15
Bloomington: Mall of America
952.858.8949, parties

The Little Gym
tinyurl.com/lp23zfo
St. Louis Park: 8223 Hwy 7
952.924.0083, parties

Lookout Ridge at Woodbury's Central Park
tinyurl.com/lawkzfo
Woodbury: 8595 Central Park Pl
651.414.3434, parties

Maple Maze—Maple Grove Community Center
tinyurl.com/mqt8nvy
Maple Grove: 12951 Weaver Lk Rd, 763.494.6500, parties
Entertainment D62 exp 12/30/15

Midtown Global Market
tinyurl.com/q2u2r6f
Minneapolis: 920 E Lk St #G10
612.872.4041, free Wee Wed free Fri family night

MN Pro Paintball
mnpropaintball.com
Burnsville: 14021 Grand Ave
952.303.5807
Lakeville: 22554 Texas Ave
952.892.1540

The Monkey House
monkeyhousemn.com
White Bear Lake: 1815 Buerkle Rd, 651.348.8233
Entertainment D81, 10/31/15
Entertainment mobile & online

Movement Lab
movementlabminneapolis.com
Minneapolis: 5155 Bloomington Ave S, 612.597.6830, classes

My Gym Children's Fitness Center
mygym.com
Eden Prairie: 6545 Flying Cloud Dr, 952.906.0028
classes, parties, *Entertainment* mobile & online

NASCAR Silicon Motor Speedway
tinyurl.com/n58y2w5
Bloomington: Mall of America
952.854.7700, parties

Nickelodeon Universe
nickelodeonuniverse.com
tinyurl.com/mq7a4ng
Bloomington: Mall of America
952.883.8600, parties, AAA
Entertainment D14—18, 12/30/15
Entertainment mobile & online
MOA *50*, 106, 231, 12/31/15
tinyurl.com/ktdyj7t , 12/31/15

Peapods
tinyurl.com/n9de6xb
St. Paul: 2290 Como Ave
651.695.5559, classes, parties
Chinook C284, 10/31/15
Chinook mobile 8/31/15

Playworks
playworksfun.com
Prior Lake: 2200 Trail of Dreams
952.445.7529, camps, parties
toddlers, adults free with child

Pump it Up
pumpitupparty.com
Eden Prairie: 7406 Washington Ave S
952.943.0052
Ham Lake: 13941 Lincoln St NE #400
763.757.9000,
Plymouth: 3500 Holly Ln N, # 65
763.553.0340
Oakdale: 7045 6th St N, 651.735.1556
Entertainment D38 12/30/15
Entertainment mobile & online date night, parties

Rainbow Play System
rainbowplay.com
Bloomington: 900 W 80th St
952.884.4040, parties, playtime

REI Rock Climbing Wall—*rei.com*
Bloomington: 750 W American Blvd
952.884.4315, classes, *Chinook* C385, 10/31/15, *Chinook* mobile 8/31/15

Sovereign Grounds
sovereigngrounds.com
Minneapolis: 813 E 48th St
612.825.6157
Entertainment mobile & online

University of Minnesota Recreation Centers
recsports.umn.edu
St. Paul: 1536 Cleveland Ave N
Minneapolis: 123 Harvard St
612.625.8790

Sky Zone Indoor Trampoline Park
skyzonesports.com
Plymouth: 13310 Industrial Park Blvd, 763.331.3511
Oakdale: 595 Hale Ave N
651.200.3383, parties, toddlers
Entertainment D65—66, 12/30/15

Triple Play Sports
tripleplaysports.biz
Prior Lake: 5832 Industrial Lane SE
952.440.3330, parties

Vertical Endeavors
verticalendeavors.com
Minneapolis: 2540 Nicollet Ave S
612.436.1470
St. Paul: 855 Phalen Blvd
651.776.1430, camps, parties
Chinook C387, 10/31/15
Chinook Mobile 8/31/15
Entertainment E114, 12/30/15
Entertainment mobile & online

Woodale Fun Zone
wooddalefunzone.com
Woodbury: 2122 Wooddale Dr
651.735.6214
Entertainment D34, 10/31/15

Zero Gravity Trampoline Park
zerogravitymn.com
Mounds View: 2292 Woodale Dr
763.219.4010
Entertainment mobile & online

Anoka County
anoka.lib.mn.us

Andover: 15200 Hanson Blvd NW
763.576.4695

Anoka: Anoka Cty History Ctr
2135 3rd Ave N, 763.421.0600

Anoka: Rum River
4201 6th Ave, 763.576.4695

Blaine: Northtown
711 Cty Rd 10 NE, 763.717.3267

Blaine: Johnsville
12461 Oak Park Blvd, 763.767.3853

Circle Pines: Centennial
100 Civic Heights Cir, 763.717.3294

Columbia Heights: 820 40th Ave NE
763.706.3690

Coon Rapids: Crooked Lake
114400 Crooked Lk Blvd, 763.576.5972

Fridley: Mississippi
410 Mississippi St NE, 763.571.1934

Ham Lake: North Central
17565 Central Ave NE, 763.434.6542

Ramsey: 75500 Sunwood Dr NW
763.576.4695

St. Francis: 3519 Bridge St NW
763.753.2131

Carver County
www.carverlib.org

Chanhassen: 7711 Kerber Blvd
952.227.1500

Chaska: 3 City Hall Plaza
952.448.3886

Chaska: 604 E 4th St, 952.361.1564

Norwood Young America
314 Elm St W, 952.467.2665

Waconia: 217 S Vine St
952.442.4714

Watertown: 309 Lewis Ave SW
952.955.2939

Dakota County
www.co.dakota.mn.us/libraries

Apple Valley: 14955 Galaxie Ave
952.891.7045

Burnsville: 1101 W Cty Rd 42
952.891.0300

Eagan: 1340 Wescott Rd
651.450.2900

Farmington: 508 3rd St
651.438.0250

Hastings: 1490 S Frontage Rd
651.438.0200

Inver Grove Heights: 8098 Blaine Ave
651.554.6840

Lakeville: 20085 Heritage Dr
952.891.0360

Rosemount: 14395 S Robert Tr
651.480.1200

South St. Paul: 106 3rd Ave N
651.554.3240

West St. Paul: 199 E Wentworth Ave
651.554.6800

Hennepin County
hclib.org

Bloomington: Oxboro
8801 Portland Ave S, 612.543.5775

Bloomington: Penn Lake
8800 Penn Ave S, 612.543.5800

Brooklyn Ctr: Brookdale, 6125
Shingle Circle Pkwy 612.543.5600

Brooklyn Park: 8600 Zane Ave N
612.543.6225

Champlin: 12154 Ensign Ave N
612.543.6250

Crystal: Rockford Road
6401 42nd Ave N, 612.543.5875

Eden Prairie: 565 Prairie Center Dr
612.543.6275

Edina: 5280 Grandview Square
612.543.6325

Edina: Southdale
7001 York Ave S, 612.543.5900

Excelsior: 343 Third St,
612.543.6350

Golden Valley: 830 Winnetka Ave
N, 612.543.6375

Hopkins: 22 11th Ave N,
612.543.6400

Long Lake, 1865 Wayzata Blvd W
612.543.6425

Maple Grove: 8001 Main St N
612.543.6450

Maple Plain: 5184 Main St E
612.543.5700

Minnetonka: 17524 Excelsior Blvd
612.543.5725

Minnetonka: Ridgedale
12601 Ridgedale Dr
612.543.8800

Mound: Westonka
2079 Commerce Blvd
612.543.6175

Osseo: 415 Central Ave
612.543.5750

Plymouth: 15700 36th Ave N
612.543.5825

Richfield: Augsburg Park
7100 Nicollet Ave
612.543.6200

Rogers: 21300 John Milless Dr
612.543.6050

St. Anthony: 2941 Pentagon Dr NE
612.543.6075

St. Bonifacius: 8624 Kennedy
Memorial Dr, 612.543.6100

St. Louis Park: 3240 Library Ln
612.543.6125

Wayzata: 620 Rice St
612.543.6150

Minneapolis
hclib.org

Central: 300 Nicollet Mall
612.543.8000
Childish Films
tinyurl.com/krbd2w3

East Lake: 2727 E Lake St
612.543.8425

Franklin: 1314 E Franklin Ave
612.543.6925

Hosmer: 347 E 36th St
612.543.6900

Linden Hills: 2900 W 43rd St
612.543.6825

Nokomis: 5100 34th Ave S
612.543.6800

North Regional: 1315 Lowry Ave N
612.543.8450

Northeast: 2200 Central Ave NE
612.543.6775

Pierre Bottineau: 55 Broadway St NE
612.543.6850

Roosevelt: 4026 28th Ave S
612.543.6700

Southeast: 1222 4th St SE
612.543.6725

Sumner: 611 Van White Memorial
Blvd 612.543.6875

Walker: 2880 Hennepin Ave
612.543.8400

Washburn: 5244 Lyndale Ave S
612.543.8375

Webber Park: 4203 Webber Pkwy
612543.6750

Ramsey County
rclreads.org

Maplewood: 3025 Southlawn Dr
651.724.6003

Mounds View: 2576 Cty Rd 10
612.724.6004

North St. Paul: 2300 N St. Paul Dr
651.724.6005

Roseville: 2180 N Hamline Ave
651.724.6001

Shoreview: 4570 N Victoria St
651.724.6006

White Bear Lake: 4698 Clark Ave
651.724.6007

St. Paul
sppl.org
Bookmobile
tinyurl.com/lmqom5k

Arlington Hills: 1200 Payne Ave
651.632.3870

Dayton's Bluff: 645 E 7th St
651.793.1699

George Latimer Central: 90 W 4th
St 651.266.7000

Hamline Midway: 1558 W
Minnehaha Ave, 651.642.0293

Hayden Heights: 1456 White Bear
Ave, 651.793.3934

Highland Park: 1974 Ford Pkwy
651.695.3700

Merriam Park: 1831 Marshall Ave
651.642.0385

Rice Park: 1011 Rice St
651.558.2223

Riverview: 1 E George St
651.292.6626

Rondo: 461 N Dale St
651.266.7400

St. Anthony Park: 2245 Como Ave
651.642.0411

Sun Ray: 2105 Wilson Ave
651.501.6300

West 7th: 265 Oneida St
651.298.5516

Debra S. Fish: 10 Yorkton Ct
651.641.0305

Debra S. Fish (Minneapolis)
2021 East Hennepin Ave #250
651.641.0305

Scott County
scott.lib.mn.us

Belle Plaine: 125 W Main
952.873.6767

Elko New Market: 110 J. Roberts
Way, 952.496.8030

Jordan: 275 Creek Lane S
952.496.8050

New Prague: 400 E Main St
952.758.2391

Prior Lake: 16210 Eagle Creek Ave SE
952.447.3375

Savage: 13090 Alabama Ave S
952.707.1770

Shakopee: 235 Lewis St S
952.233.9590

Washington County
tinyurl.com/lemubbp

Bayport: 582 N 4th St
651.275.4416

Cottage Grove: Park Grove
7900 Hemingway Ave

Forest Lake: Hardwood Creek
19955 Forest Rd N
651.275.7300

Lakeland: Valley
380 St. Croix Tr S
651.436.5882

Mahtomedi: Wildwood
763 Stillwater Rd
651.426.2042

Oakdale: 1010 Heron Ave N
651.730.0504

Stillwater: 224 3rd St N
651.275.4338

Woodbury: RH Stafford
8595 Central Park Pl
651.731.1320

Edina Art Center
edinaartcenter.com
Edina: 4701 W 64th St
952.903.5780
classes, camps

Heartfelt
heartfeltonline.com
Minneapolis: 4306 Upton Ave S
612.877.8090
camps, classes, parties

Mr. Little Guy
mrlittleguy.com
Minneapolis: Lake Harriet
write a letter to Mr. Little Guy and
check back in a few weeks to read
his response

Minnesota Landscape Arboretum
arboretum.umn.edu
arboretum.umn.edu
Chaska: 3675 Arboretum Dr
952.443.1400, AAA, *Chinook* C188
10/31/15, *Chinook* mobile 8/31/15
Entertainment D44 exp 12/30/15
Entertainment mobile & online
12 and under free with adult
entrance, free Jan—March, free
3rd Thurs Apr—Dec after 4:30 PM

Little Enchantments
littleenchantments.com
Minneapolis: 5013 Ewing Ave S
612.746.4040
fairy garden classes

**Maureen Carlson's Center
for Creative Arts**
tinyurl.com/klr3mbe
Jordan: 102 Water St
952.492.3260

Pahl's Market
tinyurl.com/n4vjc2r
Apple Valley: 6885 160th St W
952.431.4345

Tonkadale Greenhouse
tonkadale.com
Minnetonka: 3739 Tonkawood Rd
952.938.6480

Visiting *The Little Guy's* home near Lake Harriet

AMC—*amctheatres.com*
Coon Rapids: 10051 Woodcrest Dr NW, 763.757.6233
Eden Prairie: 8251 Flying Cloud Dr #4000, 952.656.0010
Edina: 400 Southdale Center 952.920.9595
Inver Grove Heights: 5567 Bishop Ave, 651.453.1916
Maple Grove: 12575 Elm Creek Blvd N, 763.494.0379
Roseville: 850 Rosedale Center 651.604.9344, AAA

Buffalo Cinema
tinyurl.com/lemeabq
Buffalo: 100 1st Ave NE
763.682.3000

Great Clips Imax Theatre
imax.com/Minnesota
Apple Valley: 12000 Zoo Blvd
952.431.4629, parties
tinyurl.com/mwfnmce
tinyurl.com/keu9g5e, 12/31/15

Heights Theater
heightstheater.com
Columbia Heights: 3951 Central Ave NE, 763.788.9079
parties, *Chinook* mobile 8/31/15, MPR, TPT

Mann Theatres
manntheatresmn.com, AAA
Champlin: 11500 Theatre Dr
763.712.9955
Hopkins: 1118 Main St
952.931.7992
Plymouth: 3400 Vicksburg Ln
763.551.0000
St. Louis Park: 5400 Excelsior Blvd
952.927.9611
St. Paul: 1830 Grand Ave
651.698.3344
St. Paul: 760 Cleveland Ave S
651.698.3085
Entertainment D2-7, 12/30/15
Entertainment mobile & online

Marcus Theatres
marcustheatres.com
Elk River: 570 Freeport
763.441.1234
Hastings: 1325 S Frontage Rd
651.438.9700
Oakdale: 5677 Hadley Ave N
651.770.4994
Rosemount: 15280 Carrousel Way
651.322.4600
Shakopee: 1116 Shakopee Twn Sq
952.445.5300
Entertainment 8—10, 12/30/15
Entertainment mobile & online

Muller Family Theatres
Delano: 4423 US Hwy 12
763.972.3587
Monticello: 9375 Deegan Ave
763.295.5007
Lakeville: 20653 Keokuk Ave
952.985.5324
East Bethel: 18635 Ulysses NE
763.434.7253
Plymouth: 9900 Shelard Pkwy
763.591.5921
Rogers: 13692 Rogers Dr
763.428.3846
White Bear Township: 1180 Cty Rd J
651.653.3243, parties

New Hope Cinema Grill
newhopecinemagrill.com
New Hope: 2749 Winnetka Ave N
763.417.0017, parties, AAA

Oak Street Theatre
mnfilmarts.org/oakstreet/
Minneapolis: 309 Oak Street SE
612.331.3134

OMNITHEATER
smm.org
St. Paul: 120 W Kellogg Blvd
651.221.9444

Pepito's Parkway Theater
theparkwaytheater.com
Minneapolis: 4817 Chicago Ave
612.822.3030, MPR

Regal Entertainment Group
regmovies.com
Eagan: 2055 Cliff Rd
651.452.8329
Minneapolis: 6420 Camden Ave N
844.462.7342
AARP, *Entertainment D1*, 12/30/15

Riverview Theater
riverviewtheater.com
Minneapolis: 3800 42nd Ave S
612.729.7369

St. Anthony Main Theatre
stanthonymaintheatre.com
Minneapolis: 115 SE Main St
612.331.4724

Showplace ICON Theatre
showplaceicon.com
St. Louis Park: 1625 West End Blvd
763.568.0375

Theatres at Mall of America
theatersmoa.com
Bloomington: Mall of America
952.883.8901, *MOA 58* 12/31/15,
free family, sensory sensitive, &
toddler movies
tinyurl.com/m6wzgyd
tinyurl.com/k3m5z8x
tinyurl.com/loaa8dm

Vali Hi Drive In Theatre
valihi.com
Lake Elmo: 11260 Hudson Blvd N
651.436.7464

Carpenter St. Croix Valley Nature Center
carpenternaturecenter.org
Hastings: 12805 St. Croix Tr
651.437.4359
Hudson, WI: 300 E Cove Rd

Dodge Nature Center
dodgenaturecenter.org
West St. Paul: 365 W Marie Ave
651.455.4531, parties

Eastman Nature Center
tinyurl.com/ahojn88
Dayton: 13351 Elm Creek Dr
763.694.7700, parties

The Brickyards of St. Paul
tinyurl.com/nxsw55f
St. Paul: 950 Lilydale Rd
651.632.5111

Harriet Alexander Nature Center
tinyurl.com/q39d6ul
Roseville: 2520 North Dale St
651.765.4262, parties

Lowry Nature Center
tinyurl.com/q7ogzd4
Victoria: 7025 Victoria Dr
763.694.7650, parties

Maplewood Nature Center & Preserves
tinyurl.com/lcyfjku
Maplewood: 2659 E 7th St
651.249.2170, parties

National Eagle Center
nationaleaglecenter.org
Wabasha: 50 Pembroke Ave
651.565.4989, MPR

Richardson Nature Center
tinyurl.com/83slbvw
Bloomington: 8737 E Bush Lake Rd
763.694.7676, parties

Sierra Club North Star Chapter
northstar.sierraclub.org
Minneapolis: 2327 E Franklin Ave, Ste 1
612.659.9124

Silverwood Park
tinyurl.com/oxzho7z
St. Anthony: 2500 Cty Rd E
763.694.7707, parties

Springbrook Nature Center
springbrooknaturecenter.org
Fridley: 100 85th Ave N
763.572.3588, parties

Tamarack Nature Center
tinyurl.com/pz3nqb2
White Bear Lake: 5287 Otter Lake Rd
651.407.5350, parties

Warner Nature Center
warnernaturecenter.org
Marine on St. Croix: 15375 Norell Ave N
651.433.2427, camps, parties

Westwood Hills Nature Center
tinyurl.com/kl3fw6b
St. Louis Park: 8300 W Franklin Ave
952.924.2544, parties

Woodlake Nature Center in winter

Aamodt's Apple Farm
aamodtsapplefarm.com
Stillwater: 6428 Manning Ave N
651.439.3127

Afton Apple Orchards
aftonapple.com
Afton: 14421 S 90th St
651.436.8385

The Apple House
dumasapplehouse.com
Long Lake: 3025 W Wayzata Blvd
612.473.9538

Apple Jack Orchards
applejackorchards.com
Delano: 4875 37th St SE
763.972.6673

Applewood Orchard
applewoodorchard.com
Lakeville: 22702 Hamburg Ave
952.985.5425

Axdahl's Garden Farm & Greenhouse
axdahlfarms.com
Stillwater: 7452 Manning Ave
651.439.3134

Bachman's
bachmans.com
Apple Valley: 7955 W 150th St
952.431.2242
Eden Prairie: 770 Prairie Ctr Dr
952.941.7700
Fridley: 8200 University Ave NE
763.786.8200
Maplewood: 2600 White Bear Ave
651.770.0531
Minneapolis: 6010 Lyndale Ave S
612.861.7600
Plymouth: 10050 6th Ave N
763.541.1188

Berry Hill Farm
berryhillfarm.com
Anoka: 6510 185th Ave NW
763.753.5891

The Beez Kneez
thebeezkneezdelivery.com
Minneapolis: 2204 Minnehaha Ave
612.990.9770, *Chinook* C446
10/31/15, *Chinook* mobile 8/31/15

Carpenter St. Croix Valley Nature Ctr
carpenternaturecenter.org
Hastings: 12805 St. Croix Tr
Hudson, WI: 300 E. Cove Rd
651.437.4359, parties

Fischer's Croix Farm
fischerscroixfarmorchard.com
Hastings: 12971 St. Croix Tr S
612.437.7126

Deardoff Orchards & Vineyards
deardorfforchards.com
Waconia: 8350 Parley Lk Rd
952.442.1885

Deer Lake Orchard
deerlakeorchard.com
Buffalo: 1903 10th St SW
763.682.4284

Dundee Nursery
dundeenursery.com
Plymouth: 16800 Hwy 55
763.559.4016

Egg Plant
eggplantsupply.com
St. Paul: 1771 Selby Ave
651.645.0818

Emma Krumbee's
emmakrumbees.com
Belle Plaine: 311 Enterprise Dr E
952.873.3006

Eveland Family Farm
evelandfamilyfarm.com
Andover: 2575 Andover Blvd
763.755.5123

Gale Woods Farm
tinyurl.com/yzmbb9x
Minnetrista: 7210 Cty Rd 110 W
763.694.2001

Gertens
gertens.com
Inver Grove Heights, 5500 Blaine Ave
651.450.1501

Green Valley Greenhouse
gvgh.com
Ramsey: 6530 Green Valley Rd
763.753.1621

Homestead Orchard
Maple Plain: 1080 Cty Rd 92 N
763.479.3186

Klingelhutz Pumpkins
tinyurl.com/oej9buy
Chanhassen: Hwy 212 & Hwy 101
952.442.2515

Knapton's Raspberries, Apples & Pumpkins
knaptons.org
Greenfield: 5775 State Hwy 55
763.479.1184

Luceline Orchard
lucelineorchard.com
Watertown: 2755 Rose Ave
612.817.6229

MacKinnon's Apple Creek Orchard
Lakeville: 25526 Pillsbury Ave
612.469.1851

McDougall's Apple Junction
apple-junction.com
Hastings: 14325 110th St S
651.480.4701

Minnetonka Orchards
minnetonkaorchards.com
Minnetrista: 6530 Cty Road 26
763.479.3191

Orchards & Nurseries

Minnesota Landscape Arboretum
arboretum.umn.edu
Chaska: 3675 Arboretum Dr
952.443.1400
AAA, *Chinook* C188 10/31/15
Chinook mobile 8/31/15
Entertainment D44 exp 12/30/15
Entertainment mobile & and nline
12 and under free with adult entrance
Free Jan—March, Free 3rd Thurs
Apr—Dec after 4:30 PM

Otten Bros Inc
ottenbros.com
Long Lake: 2350 W Wayzata Blvd
952.473.5425

Packer Family Farms
packerfarms.com
Andover: 16029 Round Lake Blvd
763.427.7207

Pahl's Market
pahls.com
Apple Valley: 6885 160th St W
952.431.4345

Pine Tree Orchard
pinetreeappleorchard.com
White Bear Lake: 450 Apple Orchard
Rd, 651.429.7202

Pleasant Valley
pleasantvalleyorchard.com
Shafer: 17325 Pleasant Valley Rd
651.257.9159

Sargent's Nursery
sargentsnursery.com
Red Wing: 37352 N Service Dr
651.388.3847

Shady Acres Herb Farm
shadyacres.com
Chaska: 7815 Hwy 212
952.466.3391

Southview Garden
southviewgardencenter.com
West St. Paul: 50 Crusader Ave E
651.455.6669

**Sponsel's Minnesota
Harvest Apple Orchard**
minnesotaharvest.net
Jordan: 8251 Old Hwy 169 Blvd
952.492.2785

Sunnyside Gardens
sunnyside-gardens.com
Minneapolis: 3723 W 44th St
612.926.2654
Chinook C457, 10/31/15

Tangletown Gardens
tangletowngardens.com
Minneapolis: 5353 Nicollet Ave
612.822.4769
Chinook C458, 10/31/15

Tonkadale
tonkadale.com
Minnetonka: 3739 Tonkawood Rd
952.938.6480

Thompson's Hillcrest Orchard
hillcrestorchard.org
Elko: 6271 250th St E
952.461.2055

Victoria Valley
victoriavalleyorchard.com
Shoreview: 4304 N Victoria St
651.484.4500

Wagner Greenhouses
wagnergreenhouses.com
Minneapolis: 6024 Penn Ave
612.922.9601
Chinook C461-462, 10/31/15
Chinook mobile 8/31/15

Waldoch Farm Garden Center
waldochfarm.com
Lino Lakes: 8174 Lake Dr
651.780.1207

Whistling Well Farm
whistlingwellfarm.com
Hastings: 8973 St Croix Tr S
651.998.0301

Parks & Playgrounds

PARKS

Mississippi National River and Recreation Area
nps.gov/miss
St. Paul: 120 W Kellogg Blvd
651.290.4160

U.S. Fish and Wildlife Services MN Valley National Wildlife Refuge and Recreation Area
tinyurl.com/nfrf5p8
Bloomington: 3815 American Blvd
952.854.5900

MN Department of Natural Resources
dnr.state.mn.us, mndnr.gov/ parksandtrails, mndnr.gov/ican
651.296.6157, fee-free week
tinyurl.com/psdy36, programs

Grand Rounds National Scenic Byway
tinyurl.com/ok7ptrz
612.230.6400

Anoka County Parks
anokacountyparks.com
763.757.3920

Carver County Parks
www.co.carver.mn.us/parks/
952.466.5650

Dakota County Parks
dakotacounty.us/parks
651.437.3191, parties

Ramsey County Parks & Recreation
tinyurl.com/bubg443
651.748.2500

Scott County
www.co.scott.mn.us
tinyurl.com/lpej4qv
763.559.9000, parties

Three Rivers Park District
threeriversparkdistrict.org
763.559.9000
Chinook C229, 10/31/15
Chinook mobile 8/31/15

Washington County Parks
co.washington.mn.us
651.430.6000

City Parks and Trails Minneapolis Park and Recreation Board
minneapolisparks.org
612.230.6400

St. Paul Parks and Recreation
ci.stpaul.mn.us/parks
651.266.6400

PLAYGROUNDS

The Giggle Factory
thegigglefactorykids.com
Hudson, WI: 2007 O'Neil Rd
715.386.6639

Hyland Play Area "Chutes & Ladders"
tinyurl.com/osw8j5o
Bloomington: 10145 Bush Lake Rd
763.694.7687

Rumbling River
tinyurl.com/low8wzr
Farmington: 17 Elm St
651.280.6800

Teddybear Park
tinyurl.com/nto5mtk
Stillwater: 2nd St S & Nelson St
651.430.8800

Westview Acres
tinyurl.com/low8wzr
Farmington: 50 Hickory St
651.280.6800

Teddybear Park in Stillwater

Performing Arts

Actors Theatre of Minnesota
actorsmn.org
651.290.2290

Anoka-Ramsey College Theatre
tinyurl.com/odrcc7d
Coon Rapids: 11200 Mississippi
Blvd NW
763.433.1100

Applause Community Theater
act-mn.org
Lakeville: 20965 Holyhoke Ave
952.985.4640

Artists to Go
compas.org
St. Paul: 75 5th St W, #304
651.292.3259

**Bloomington Theatre
and Art Center**
tinyurl.com/l9ae4rn
Bloomington: 1800 W Old
Shakopee Rd
952.563.8575

Broadway Across America
minneapolis.broadway.com
800.859.7469

Ames Center
ames-center.com
Burnsville: 12600 Nicollet Ave
952.895.4685, parties

The Cedar Cultural Center
thecedar.org
Minneapolis: 416 Cedar Ave S
612.338.2674

Chanhassen Dinner Theater
chanhassentheaters.com
Chanhassen: 501 W 78th St
952.934.1525, camps, AAA
Chinook C167-168, 10/31/15
Chinook mobile 8/31/15
bloomington-coupons.com

**Chaska Community
Center Theater**
chaskacommunitycenter.com
Chaska: 1661 Park Ridge Dr
952.448.5633

Chaska Valley Family Theatre
cvft.org
Chaska: 1661 Park Ridge Dr
952.448.5633, MACT

Children's Theatre Company
childrenstheatre.org
Minneapolis: 2400 3rd Ave S
612.874.0400
AAA, *Chinook* C203 10/31/15, MPR

Circus Juventas
circusjuventas.org
St. Paul: 1270 Montreal Ave
651.699.8229
camps, parties

Civic Orchestra of Minneapolis
civicorchestrampls.org
612.332.4842

Classical Ballet Academy
summerdancecamp.com
St. Paul: 249 4th St E
Woodbury: 7650 Currell Blvd
651.222.7919

Continental Ballet Company
continentalballet.com
Bloomington: 1800 W Old Shakopee
Rd, 952.563.8562

Contemporary Performance Works
offleasharea.org
Minneapolis: 3540 34th Ave S

**Coon Rapids Campus
Performing Arts Center**
tinyurl.com/k7ubmxz
Coon Rapids: 11200 Mississippi Blvd
NW, 763.433.1100

The Cowles Center
thecowlescenter.org
Minneapolis: 528 Hennepin Ave
612.206.3636
tinyurl.com/keu9g5e 12/31/15

Dakota Valley Symphony & Chorus
dakotavalleysymphony.org
952.895.4680

Encore Wind Ensemble
encorewind.com, 952.217.0121

Ethnic Dance Theatre
ethnicdancetheatre.com
763.545.1333

Exultate—*exultate.org*
Eagan: 651.707.0727, MPR

From Age to Age
fromagetoage.org, MPR

**Gilbert & Sullivan Very
Light Opera Company**
gsvloc.org, 651.255.6947

Gremlin Theatre
gremlin-theatre.org
Minneapolis: 711 W Franklin Ave
651.228.7008

Guthrie Theater—*guthrietheater.org*
Minneapolis: 818 S 2nd St
612.377.2224, *Chinook* C205 322
10/31/15, *Chinook Mobile* 8/31/15

**Harmony Theatre Company
& School**—*harmonytheatre.org*
St. Louis Park: 6121 Excelsior Blvd
763.442.1628

Hennepin Theatre District
hennepintheatredistrict.org
Minneapolis: 615 Hennepin Ave
#140, 612.339.7007, MPR

The Historic Mounds Theatre
moundstheatre.org
St. Paul: 1029 Hudson Rd
651.772.2253

Praise for *The Mindfulness Toolbox*

"This is a must-have book for every therapist using mindfulness approaches with clients. From the 10 'Tips' thru the 40 'Tools', Donald Altman shares his considerable wisdom, along with a sense of respect for both the client—and the therapist. At the same time, the material is presented in a light and very usable style, from the clear outlines to the many client handouts."

—**Jean L. Kristeller, Ph.D., Research and clinical psychologist, and developer of Mindfulness-Based Eating Awareness Training (MB-EAT)**

"The ceaselessly creative Donald Altman, in his never-ending quest to make mindfulness practice accessible to anyone motivated to learn it, has once again broached new ground in elaborating simple, useful techniques for applying mindfulness in everyday life. *The Mindfulness Toolbox* is a veritable wonderland of user-friendly implements of mindfulness practice, all laid out to maximize a new (and maybe not-so-new) practitioner's ability to effectively use applied mindfulness. *The Mindfulness Toolbox* will be a tremendous aid and benefit to all people who practice and teach mindfulness."

—**Jeffrey M. Schwartz, MD, author of *Brain Lock and You Are Not Your Brain***

"Much like any healing prescription, *The Mindfulness Toolbox* skillfully reduces pain and fosters balance by getting to the root cause of the symptoms. If you want to expand your mindfulness repertoire, you won't find a more complete and practical set of key techniques, handouts, and ideas. You'll even be guided as to which tools fit together, such as tools for sensing the body, tools for meditation, and tools for getting into the present moment. With a large dose of awareness, clarity, precision, simplicity, and insight, Donald Altman has given us a potent and worthwhile medicine for inviting well-being, acceptance, and inner peace."

—**Paul Harrison, creator and producer of The Mindfulness Movie, and author of *Where's My Zen?* and *The Ten Paradoxes: The Science of Where's My Zen?***

"Mindfulness has swept through the mental health profession in the past several decades and plays a major role in important modalities such as DBT, ACT, Mindfulness-Based Cognitive Therapy for Depression, Mindfulness-Based Relapse Prevention and others. Whether or not you are trained in any of these modalities, *The Mindfulness Toolbox* by Donald Altman is the resource you need to strengthen your use of mindfulness with a wide variety of clients. Altman is an experienced and loving guide to lead you through the mindfulness landscape. His new book presents a comprehensive set of highly practical, effective techniques, tools and handouts that will enable you to skillfully utilize mindfulness in your clinical work. The easy-to-use interventions for anxiety, depression, stress and pain are described in clear language that reflects the kindness and beauty of mindfulness. *The Mindfulness Toolbox* will not only improve your effectiveness with clients, it will also enable you to more fully integrate into your personal life the emotional, psychological and spiritual wealth offered by mindfulness practice. If you have any interest in mindfulness, you should have *The Mindfulness Toolbox* as a resource."

—**Terry Fralich, LPC, JD, author of *The Five Core Skills of Mindfulness* and *Cultivating Lasting Happiness***

"*The Mindfulness Toolbox* is a treasure trove of resources for healing and belongs in every clinician's office. It teaches simple, effective ways to reduce suffering and increase happiness. Well worth reading!"

—**Mary NurrieStearns, author of *Yoga For Anxiety, Yoga For Emotional Trauma,* and *Yoga Mind, Peaceful Mind***

"Donald Altman's newest book, *The Mindfulness Toolbox,* is an important work for how it will reduce emotional and physical suffering in the world. Highly practical and well-organized, the book tackles the key areas of stress, anxiety, depression, and pain. The evident care and attention given to the guided scripts and handouts will help build the therapeutic relationship with patients—all the while guiding them gently and persistently toward a more expansive awareness and a deepened sense of self-compassion and self-acceptance. I highly recommend it."

—**Christopher Kennedy Lawford, best-selling author,** *Symptoms of Withdrawal,* *Recover to Live,* **and** *What Addicts Know*

"In an era of high popularity for anything labeled with the word 'Mindfulness,' Altman has written a user-friendly and practical book that is as fun to read as it is helpful. He provides great handouts and suggestions for how to describe mindfulness to clients so that they can gain peace of mind when feeling anxious and optimism in the face of depression. Highly recommended."

—**John B. Arden, PhD, author of the** *Brain Bible*

"There is an old Russian fable about a swan, a pike and a crawfish pulling a horse cart in three different directions, with a predictable result: the cart is hopelessly stuck. Sometimes I think of the field of psychotherapy as too being pulled in all kinds of different directions. Each school of thought, each wave of thinking, each clinical breakthrough not only moves the field along some relative continuum of evolution, but also asunder. The novelty junkies that we all are, we don't miss a beat: we rush to update and to upgrade our clinical software with each CEU we earn. Clinician-authors such Donald Altman pull the field back together. They hold it grounded and unified around such ancient centers of therapeutic gravity as awareness and mindfulness. Altman's collection of tips and tools on how to introduce clients to the know-how of mindfulness has a powerfully anchoring force of field-tested clinical wisdom. Each of Altman's 50 mindfulness tips is a spoke on a wheel of wellbeing. Roll with it, clinician, if you feel professionally stuck."

—**Pavel Somov, Ph.D., author of** *Anger Management Jumpstart,* *Present Perfect* **and** *Eating the Moment*

"Donald Altman's new book, The Mindfulness Toolbox brings you practical, wise, and helpful techniques from a seasoned expert. With an easy-going writing style, Altman gives tips for therapists and clients plus clear exercises in every chapter for overcoming common psychological problems mindfully. He also gives useful handouts to lead clients into the experience. But the book reaches deeper, as Altman communicates the essence of mindfulness through classic stories and his own profound understandings from years of personal practice and teaching. The therapist already using mindfulness will find many ideas and techniques, and those new to mindfulness will be well guided. We recommend this book to anyone who would like to integrate this important, evidence-based method into his or her treatments, and to those who would like to deepen their own practice."

—**C. Alexander Simpkins, PhD and Annellen M. Simpkins, PhD, PESI presenters, clinicians, and authors of 28 books including** *The Yoga and Mindfulness Therapy Workbook,* *The Tao of Bipolar: Using Meditation and Mindfulness to Bring Balance and Peace,* *Zen Meditation in Psychotherapy, Meditation and Yoga in Psychotherapy,* *Neuroscience for Clinicians,* **and** *The Dao of Neuroscience*

History Theatre
historytheatre.com
St. Paul: 30 East 10th St
651.292.4323
Chinook C207, 10/31/15
Chinook mobile 8/31/15

Hopkins Center for the Arts
hopkinsartscenter.com
Hopkins: 1111 Main St
952.979.1100, parties, MPR

HUGE Improv Theater
hugetheater.com
Minneapolis: 3037 Lyndale Ave S
612.412.4243, MPR

Illusion Theatre
illusiontheater.org
Minneapolis: 528 Hennepin Ave
612.339.4944 *Chinook* C208,
10/31/15, *Chinook* mobile
8/31/15

**In the Heart of the Beast Puppet
& Mask Theatre**—*hobt.org*
Minneapolis: 1500 E Lake St
612.721.2535, parties, TPT

**Interact Center for Visual
& Performing Arts**
interactcenter.com
St. Paul: 1860 Minnehaha Ave W
612.209.3575

Jungle Theater
jungletheater.com
Minneapolis: 2951 Lyndale Ave S
612.822.7063, MPR
Chinook Book C209, 10/31/15
Chinook mobile 8/31/15

Lakeville Area Arts Center
tinyurl.com/yexr7c9
Lakeville: 20965 Holyhoke Ave
952.985.4400

Lakeshore Players Theatre
lakeshoreplayers.com
White Bear Lake: 4820 Stewart
Ave, 651.429.5674, MPR

Lundstrum Center
lundstrumcenter.org
Minneapolis: 1617 N 2nd St
612.521.2600, camps

Lyric Arts Main Street Stage
lyricarts.org
Anoka: 420 E Main St
763.422.1838, MACT, MPR

MacPhail Center for Music
macphail.org, 612.321.0100
Apple Valley: 14750 Cedar Ave S
Chanhassen: 470 W 78th St
Golden Valley: 6125 Olson Mem
Hwy, 763.279.4200
Minneapolis: 501 2nd St S
White Bear Lake: 1616 Birch Lk
Ave, free family music series,
tinyurl.com/kllta9u, camps, classes
Chinook C174—176, 10/31/15
Chinook mobile 8/31/15

Midwest Youth Dance Theatre
mydtdance.com
Falcon Heights: 1557 W
Larpenteur Ave, 651.644.2438

Minneapolis Convention Center
tinyurl.com/7arahay
Minneapolis: 1301 2nd Ave S
612.335.6000

Minneapolis Musical Theatre
aboutmmt.org
Minneapolis: 24 Hennepin Ave
612.373.5665

**Minnesota Association of
Community Theatres**
mact.net

Minnesota Boychoir
boychoir.org
St. Paul: 75 West 5th St
651.292.3219, camps

Minnesota Dance Theatre
mndance.org
612.338.0627, classes

Minnesota Chorale
mnchorale.org, 612.333.4866

**Minnesota Jewish Theatre
Company**
mnjewishtheatre.org
651.647.4315

Minnesota Opera
mnopera.org
Minneapolis: 620 N 1st St
612.333.6669, AAA, *Chinook* C211
10/31/15, *Chinook* mobile 8/31/15
Entertainment D120, 12/30/15
Entertainment mobile & online, MPR

Minnesota Orchestra
mnorch.org
Minneapolis: 1111 Nicollet Mall
612.371.5656, Target Free Families
tinyurl.com/oq7qxpw
Chinook C212, 10/31/15
Chinook mobile 8/31/15

**Minnesota Public Radio's
Fitzgerald Theatre**
fitzgeraldtheater.publicradio.org
St. Paul: 10 Exchange St E
651.290.1200

Mixed Blood Theatre
mixedblood.com
Minneapolis: 1501 4th St S
612.338.6131

The Mystery Café
themysterycafe.com
763.566.2583

The National Lutheran Choir
nlca.com
Minneapolis: 528 Hennepin Ave, #302
612.722.2301, MPR

New Century Theatre
tinyurl.com/6rpxzgm
Minneapolis: 615 Hennepin Ave
612.455.9501

Normandale Community College Theatre
tinyurl.com/qecgdpc
Bloomington: 9700 France Ave S
952.487.7462

Old Log Theater
oldlog.com
Greenwood: 5185 Meadville St
952.474.5951, AAA, MPR

Open Eye
openeyetheatre.org
Minneapolis: 506 E 24th St
612.874.6338

Oratorio Society of Minnesota
oratorio.org
St. Paul, 651.488.8902, TPT

Ordway Center
ordway.org
St. Paul: 345 Washington St
651.224.4222

Orpheum Theatre
tinyurl.com/78pa4x4
Minneapolis: 910 Hennepin Ave
800.982.2787, AAA

O'Shaughnessy Auditorium
oshaughnessy.stkate.edu
St. Paul: 2004 Randolph Ave
651.690.6700, MPR

O'Shea Irish Dance
osheairishdance.com
St. Paul: 836 Prior Ave
612.722.7000, camps

Pantages Theatre
tinyurl.com/lgtccb7
Minneapolis: 710 Hennepin Ave
612.339.7007, AAA

Park Square Theatre
parksquaretheatre.org
St. Paul: 20 West 7th Pl
651.291.7005, MPR, TPT

Penumbra Theatre Company
penumbratheatre.org
St. Paul: 270 N Kent St
651.224.3180

Pillsbury House Theatre
pillsburyhousetheatre.org
Minneapolis: 3501 Chicago Ave
612.825.0459

The Playwright's Center
pwcenter.org
Minneapolis: 2301 Franklin Ave E
612.332.7481

Plymouth Playhouse
plymouthplayhouse.com
Plymouth: 2705 Annapolis Lane
763.553.1600
AAA, *Entertainment* D43, 12/30/15,
Entertainment mobile & online
tinyurl.com/ktdyj7t 12/31/15

Rosetown Playhouse
rosetownplayhouse.org
Roseville: 2660 Civic Center Dr
651.792.7414 x2

Roy Wilkins Auditorium
tinyurl.com/m3l4ecx
St. Paul: 175 W Kellogg Blvd
651.265.4800

St. Louis Park Community Band
slpband.org

The St. Paul Chamber Orchestra
thespco.org
St. Paul: 408 St. Peter St
651.291.1144, free activities
before family concerts, parties
Chinook C214, 10/31/15
Chinook mobile 8/31/15

St. Paul Ballet
spcballet.org
Chinook C215, 10/31/15
Chinook mobile 8/31/15
St. Paul: 655 Fairview Ave
651.690.1588

The Singers—*singersmca.org*
Minneapolis: 528 Hennepin Ave
#303, 651.917.1948, MPR

The Rose Ensemble
roseensemble.org
St. Paul: 75 W 5th St, #314
651.225.4340, MPR

James Sewell Ballet—*jsballet.org*
Minneapolis: 528 Hennepin Ave
#215, 612.672.0480

The Schubert Club
www.schubert.org
St. Paul: 202 Landmark Center
75 5th St, 651.292.3267

Shakespeare and Company
tinyurl.com/85rg8g2
White Bear Lake: 3300 Century Ave
N, 651.779.5818

Southern Theater
southerntheater.org
Minneapolis: 1420 Washington Ave
612.340.1725

Stages Theatre Company
stagestheatre.org
Hopkins: 1111 Mainstreet
952.979.1111, parties, *Chinook*
C216, 10/31/15, *Chinook*
mobile 8/31/15, *Entertainment*
mobile & online, TPT

State Theatre
tinyurl.com/ny3abry, AAA
Minneapolis: 805 Hennepin Ave
612.339.7007

Steppingstone Theatre
steppingstonetheatre.org
St. Paul: 55 Victoria St N
651.225.9265, camps

Tapestry Folkdance Center
tapestryfolkdance.org
Minneapolis: 3748 Minnehaha Ave
S, 612.722.2914

Theater in the Woods
tinyurl.com/lsqh3ad
Eagan: 1220 Diffley Rd
651.454.9412

Theatre in the Round
theatreintheround.org
Minneapolis: 245 Cedar Ave
612.333.3010
MPR, *Chinook* C217 exp 10/31/15

Troupe America
troupeamerica.com
Minneapolis: 3313 Republic Ave
612.333.3302

Theatre Unbound
theatreunbound.com
612.721.1186
TPT

Twin Cities Gay Men's Chorus
tcgmc.org
612.339.7664
MPR

**University of Minnesota
Performing Arts**
artsquarter.umn.edu
612.624.9839
music.umn.edu
612.624.5740
northrop.umn.edu
612.624.2345
Chinook mobile 8/31/15

Vocal Essence
vocalessence.org
Minneapolis: 1900 Nicollet Ave
612.547.1451, AAA, MPR

Yellow Tree Theatre
yellowtreetheatre.com
Osseo: 320 5th Ave SE
763.493.8733
parties

Young Artists Initiative
youngartistsmn.org
St. Paul: 463 Maria Ave
651.222.5437

Youth Performance Co
youthperformanceco.com
Minneapolis: 3338 University Ave SE
612.623.9080
Entertainment mobile & online

Walker Art Center
walkerart.org
Minneapolis: 1750 Hennepin Ave
612.375.7600

Zenon Dance Co and School
zenondance.org
Minneapolis: 1900 Nicollet Ave
612.623.9180
Chinook mobile 8/31/15

Bakken Library & Museum of Electricity in Life
thebakken.org
Minneapolis: 3537 Zenith Ave S
612.926.3878
parties, TPT

Bell Museum of Natural History
bellmuseum.org
Minneapolis: 10 Church St SE
612.626.9660, camps, parties
Chinook C219 exp 10/31/15
Chinook mobile 8/31/15

Insect Collection
www.entomology.umn.edu
St. Paul: Department of
Entomology, University of
Minnesota, 219 Hodson Hall 1980
Follwell Ave
612.624.3636

Mad Science of Minnesota
mn.madscience.org
St. Paul: 519 Payne Ave
651.793.5721
after-school, programs, camps,
classes, parties

Science Museum of Minnesota
smm.org
St. Paul: 120 W Kellogg Blvd
651.221.9444, parties
Tues, 10 AM—12 PM, 5 and under
free with adult, smm.org/playdates

Tech Academy
techacademymn.com
Little Canada: 80 Minnesota Ave
651.486.2780
camps, parties

The Works Museum
theworks.org
Bloomington: 9740 Grand Ave S
952.888.4262, camps, parties
bloomington-coupons.com 12/31/15
Chinook C221, 10/31/15
Chinook mobile 8/31/15, TPT

STAR GAZING

Minnesota Astronomical Society
mnastro.org
Cherry Grove Observatory
Kenyon: 8485 520th St
952.467.2426
Eagle Lake Observatory
Norwood Young America: 10775
Cty Rd 33, 952.448.6082
Joseph J. Casby Observatory
Afton: 1553 Stagecoach Tr S
Metcalf Observing Field
tinyurl.com/o9r22qs

Como Planetarium
planetarium.spps.org
St. Paul: 780 W Wheelock Pkwy
651.293.5398

Eisenhower Observatory
tinyurl.com/nxoqrrd
Hopkins: 1001 Hwy 7
952.988.4070

Tate Laboratory of Physics
www.astro.umn.edu
Minneapolis: 116 Church St SE
612.624.4811

Playing and learning at The Works in Bloomington

ICE SKATING

Aldrich Ice Arena
tinyurl.com/mn6seye
Maplewood: 1850 N White Bear
Ave 651.748.2510, parties

Bielenberg Sports Center
tinyurl.com/k9mu46r
Woodbury: 4125 Radio Dr
651.714.3740

**Brooklyn Park Community
Activity Center**
tinyurl.com/modxa96
Entertainment mobile& online
Brooklyn Park: 5600 85th Ave N
763.493.8333

Burnsville Ice Center
burnsvilleicecenter.org
Burnsville: 251 Civic Center Pkwy
952.895.4651, parties, *Entertainment* mobile & online

Coon Rapids Ice Center
coonrapidsicecenter.com
Coon Rapids: 11000 Crooked Lk
Blvd 763.951.7222parties

Depot Rink
tinyurl.com/mq9l44w
Minneapolis: 225 S 3rd Ave
612.339.2253
Chinook C386, 10/31/15

Eagan Civic Arena Public Skating
tinyurl.com/lmrqmj3
Eagan: 3870 Pilot Knob Rd
651.675.5590, parties

**Guidant John Rose
MN OVAL and Arena**
tinyurl.com/plr36xq
Roseville: 2661 Civic Center Dr
651.792.7007, parties

Parade Ice Garden
tinyurl.com/mrygjym
Minneapolis: 600 Kenwood Pkwy
612.230.6527, parties

Richfield Ice Arena
tinyurl.com/n84abvv
Richfield: 636 East 66th St
612.861.9351
Entertainment D100 exp 10/31/15
Entertainment mobile & online

Roseville Ice Arena
tinyurl.com/pbc8muw
Roseville: 2661 Civic Center Dr
651.792.7007, parties

St. Louis Park Rec Center
tinyurl.com/kaddmrb
St. Louis Park: 3700 Monterey Dr
952.924.2540

**Charles M. Schulz-Highland
Arena Ice Complex**
tinyurl.com/qgkqajn
St. Paul: 800 S Snelling Ave
651.695.3768, parties

Ken Yackel West Side Arena
tinyurl.com/n7mv75n
St. Paul: 44 Isabel St E
651.748.2500, parties

ROLLER SKATING

Cheap Skate
cheapskatecr.com
Coon Rapids: 3075 Coon Rapids
Blvd NW, 763.427.8980, parties
Entertainment D95 exp 12/30/15
Entertainment mobile & online

Roller Garden
rollergarden.com
St. Louis Park: 5622 W Lake St
952.929.5518, parties

**Saints North Maplewood
Family Skate Center**
www.saintsnorth.com
Maplewood: 1818 Gervais Ct
651.770.3848, parties

Schwan Super Rink
tinyurl.com/lhtka92
Blaine: 1700 105th Ave NE
763.717.5600, parties

Skateville
skateville.com
Entertainment D102 exp 10/31/15
Entertainment Mobileand Online
Burnsville: 201 S River Ridge Cir
952.890.0988, parties

**3rd Lair Skatepark
and Skateshop**
3rdlair.com
Golden Valley: 850 Florida Ave S
763.797.5283

Woodale Fun Zone
wooddalefunzone.com
Woodbury: 2122 Wooddale Dr
651.735.6214

SKATEPARKS

Augsburg Skatepark
tinyurl.com/nejtnjn
Richfield: 70th St & Nicollet Ave

3rd Lair Skatepark
3rdlair.com
Golden Valley: 850 Florida Ave S
763.797.5283

**Minneapolis Park &
Recreation Board**
tinyurl.com/pr4zjcd

CROSS COUNTRY SKIING

Hyland Park Ski and Snowboard Area
tinyurl.com/yjjgmqg
Bloomington: 8800 Chalet Rd
763.694.7800

Landscape Arboretum
arboretum.umn.edu
Chaska: 3675 Arboretum Dr
952.443.1400, AAA

Washington County Trails
tinyurl.com/l46hlfo, 651.430.8370

Woodlake Nature Center
tinyurl.com/qzy6hnh
Richfield: 6710 Lakeshore Dr
612.861.9365

DOWN HILL SKIING

Afton Alps—aftonalps.com
Hastings: 6600 Peller Ave S
651.436.5245, parties

Buck Hill Ski Area
buckhill.com
Burnsville: 15400 Buck Hill Rd
952.435.7174

Eko Backen Snow Tubing
ekobacken.com
Scandia: 22570 Manning Tr
651.433.2422, parties, MPR

Photo courtesy Jeremy Swanson

Elm Creek Park Reserve
tinyurl.com/6veh8o4
Maple Grove: 12400 James Dean
Parkway 763.694.7894

Hyland Ski and Snowboard Area
tinyurl.com/yjjgmqg
Bloomington: 8800 Chalet Rd
763.694.7800

Welch Village Ski and Snowboard Area
welchvillage.com
Welch, 26685 Cty Rd 7 Blvd
651.258.4567

Wild Mountain—wildmountain.com
Taylors Falls: 37200 Wild Mt Rd
651.465.6315, parties

SLEDDING

Check county & city listings pages
13—14

Adams Hill Park
tinyurl.com/ll8n3rf
Richfield: 7200 Washburn Ave S
612.861.9385

Afton Alps Recreational Area
aftonalps.com
Hastings: 6600 Pellers Ave
651.436.5245, parties

Buck Hill
buckhill.com
Burnsville: 15400 Buck Hill Rd
952.435.7174

Como Park Golf Course
St. Paul: Corner of N Chelsea
& W Arlington Ave, 651.488.9673

Elm Creek Recreational Area
tinyurl.com/45sy9yx
Maple Grove: 12400 James Dean
Pkwy, 763.694.7894

Hyland Park
tinyurl.com/q6dfs8c
Bloomington: 10145 Bush Lake Rd
763.694.7687

Lyndale Farmstead Park
tinyurl.com/mz75d4
Minneapolis: 3900 Bryant Ave S
612.370.4948

Marthaler Park
tinyurl.com/qx5b4lj
West St. Paul: 625 Humboldt Ave
651.552.4100

Neil Park
tinyurl.com/ofe8fze
Burnsville: 13501 Upton Ave
952.895.4500

South Valley Park
tinyurl.com/mx3o9py
Inver Grove Heights: 2810 70th St

Staring Lake
tinyurl.com/pz8vc8g
Eden Prairie: 14800 Pioneer Tl
952.949.8300

Trapp Farm Park Snow Tubing Park
tinyurl.com/ms37bqb
Eagan: 841 Wilderness Run Rd
651.675.5511, parties

Wild Chutes Snow Tubing
wildmountain.com
Taylors Falls: 37200 Wild Mt Rd
651.465.6315, parties

Minnesota Lynx
wnba.com/lynx/
Minneapolis: 600 First Ave N
612.673.8400, AAA

Minnesota Swarm
mnswarm.com
St. Paul: Xcel Energy Center
175 Kellogg Blvd West
888.667.9276, AAA

Minnesota Timberwolves
nba.com/timberwolves/
Minneapolis: 600 First Ave N
612.673.1234, AAA

Minnesota Twins Baseball
minnesota.twins.mlb.com
Minneapolis: Target Field
1 Twins Way, 866.800.1275, AAA

Minnesota United FC Soccer
mnunitedfc.com
763.476.2237, AAA

Minnesota Wild Hockey
wild.nhl.com
St. Paul: Xcel Energy Center
175 Kellogg Blvd W
651.222.9453, AAA

Minnesota Vikings Football
vikings.com, 612.338.4537

National Sports Center
nscsports.com
Blaine: 1700 105th Ave NE
763.785.5600

St. Paul Saints
saintsbaseball.com
St. Paul: 1771 Energy Park Dr
651.644.6659, AAA

**University of Minnesota
Gopher Sports**
gophersports.com
800.846.7437
AAA, *Entertainment* mobile & online

Swimming & Splash Pads

INDOOR WATERPARKS

Edinborough
tinyurl.com/oux7cob
Edina: 7700 York Ave S
952.833.9540, season pass

Great River Water Park
tinyurl.com/d7cqeof
St. Paul: 270 Lexington Pkwy N
651.642.0650, parties

**The Grove Aquatic
& Fitness Center**
funatthegrove.com
Inver Grove Heights: 8055 Barbara
Ave, 651.450.2480, parties

Tropics Indoor Water Park
tinyurl.com/knotkhf
Shoreview: 4580 Victoria St N
651.490.4700, parties

Water Park of America
waterparkofamerica.com
Bloomington: 1700 American Blvd
E 952.854.8700, parties, AAA
Entertainment D23 exp 12/31/15
Entertainment mobile & online
MOA 265—266 exp 12/31/14, TPT

Wild Woods Waterpark
hielkriver.com/waterpark/
Elk River: 9200 Quaday Ave NE
763.656.4400, parties
Entertainment D64, 12/30/15
Entertainment mobile & online

OUTDOOR WATERPARKS

Anoka Aquatic Center
tinyurl.com/cumwk4n
Anoka: 1551 7th Ave N
763.576.2980 parties

**Apple Valley Family
Aquatic Center**
tinyurl.com/pge3r3k
Apple Valley: 14421 Johnny Cake
Ridge Rd, 952.953.2399, parties

Battle Creek Waterworks
tinyurl.com/ldk378e
Maplewood: 2401 Upper Afton Rd
651.748.2500, parties

**Bloomington Family
Aquatic Center**
tinyurl.com/pgfgwx4
Bloomington: 201 E 90th St
952.563.4634, parties

Bunker Beach Water Park
bunkerbeach.com
Coon Rapids: 701 Cty Pkwy A
763.767.2895, parties

Cascade Bay—*cascadebay.com*
Eagan: 1360 Civic Center Dr
651.675.5577, parties

Chaska Community Center
chaskacommunitycenter.com
Chaska: 1661 Park Ridge Dr
952.448.4633, parties
Entertainment mobile & online

Crystal Cove Aquatic Center
tinyurl.com/n4ekekd
Crystal: 4800 Douglas Dr N
763.531.1170, parties

Edina Aquatic Center
edinaaquaticcenter.com
Edina: 4300 66th St W
952.833.9543, parties

Hastings Family Aquatic Center
tinyurl.com/cjbg9eu
Hastings: 901 Maple St
651.480.2392, parties

Highland Park Aquatic Center
facbook.com/highlandaquatic
St. Paul: 1840 Edgcumbe Rd
651.695.3773

Jim Lupient Water Park
tinyurl.com/nry9556
Minneapolis: 1520 Johnson St NE
612.370.3989, lessons, parties

**St. Louis Park Rrecreation Center and
Outdoor Aquatic Park**
tinyurl.com/k3syrgd
St. Louis Park: 3700 Monterey Dr
952.924.2540, parties
Entertainment D53, 10/31/15
Entertainment mobile & online

Redwood Community Pool
tinyurl.com/q2rjsmg
Apple Valley: 311 Cty Rd 42
952.953.2300

Richfield Municipal Pool
tinyurl.com/mnkctoa
Richfield: 630 E 66th St
612.861.9350
Entertainment D101, 10/31/15

Valleyfair Soak City Water Park
tinyurl.com/kayjxo2
Shakopee: 1 Valleyfair Dr
952.455.6500

WADING POOLS &
SPLASH PADS

Cedarcrest Park
tinyurl.com/l4e5cg4
Bloomington: 8700 Bloomington Ave

Central Park Splash Deck
tinyurl.com/n84ukrs
St. Anthony Village: 3400 Silver Lk Rd

Como Town Splash Zone
comotown.com
St. Paul: 1301 Midway Pkwy
651.487.1212

Conway Recreation Center
tinyurl.com/3hetnya
St. Paul: 2090 Conway Ave

Emerald Park Splash Deck
tinyurl.com/n84ukrs
St. Anthony Village: 3925
Macalaster Dr

Highlands Park
tinyurl.com/oyg2pjl
Cottage Grove: 6975 Idsen Ave S

Hyland Play Area
"Chutes and Ladders"
tinyurl.com/osw8j5o
Bloomington: 101455 Bush Lk Rd

Kelley Park
tinyurl.com/o2fbpn8
Apple Valley: 6855 Fortino Street

Lake Hiawatha Splash Pad
Minneapolis: 2701 E 44th St
612.370.4930

Lakeside Commons Park & Beach
tinyurl.com/ksegpfx

Lewis Park
tinyurl.com/o9yayds
St. Paul: 882 N Marion St

Manor Park
tinyurl.com/muuyjhv
Robbinsdale: Lowry & Abbott Ave

Miller Park Splash Pad
tinyurl.com/mc6t7gq
Eden Prairie: 8200 Eden Prairie Rd

Minneapolis
tinyurl.com/la987d8
60+ wading pools and splash pads

Nicollet Commons Park
Burnsville: 12550 Nicollet Ave

Oak Hill Splash Pad
tinyurl.com/k869c3s
St. Louis Park: 3201 Rhode Island Ave

Round Lake Splash Pad
tinyurl.com/mc6t7gq
Eden Prairie: 16691 Valley View Rd

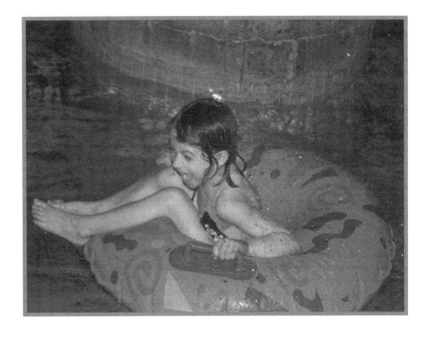

TEA TIME

Avalon Tea Room
avalontearoom.com
events, parties
White Bear Lake: 2179 4th St
651.653.3822

Lady Elegant's Team Room
ladyelegantstea.com
events, parties ages 5+
St. Paul: 2230 Carter Ave
651.646.6676
Entertainment mobile & online

Mad Hatter Tea Room
madhattertearoom.com
Anoka: 1632 S Ferry St
763.422.4160
parties, 5+ years

TOURS OF THE TWIN CITIES

Above The Falls Sports
abovethefallssports.com
Minneapolis: 120 N 3rd Ave
612.825.8983

Award-Winning City Tours
awardwinningcitytours.com
Minneapolis: 1650 W 82nd St
125, 612.929.8687, AAA
bloomington-coupons.com
12/31/15, *tinyurl.com/mddvvyt*

The Fit Tourist
thefittourist.com
Minneapolis: 800.979.337
9 & under free

The Hitching Company
thehitchingcompany.com
Minneapolis: 612.338.7777

Let's Roll Pedicabs
minneapolispedicab.com
Minneapolis: 612.558.2211

Minneapolis City By Nature
tinyurl.com/n88kzva
Minneapolis: 250 Marquette Ave S
888.676.MPLS

Paradise Charter Cruises
Minneapolis Queen
twincitiescruises.com
Excelsior: 2 Water St
Minneapolis: 2150 W River Pkwy
952.474.8058
bloomington-coupons.com 10/20/15

Pedal Pub
twincities.pedalpub.com
952.703.9000

Padelford Riverboats
riverrides.com
St. Paul: Harriet Island
651.227.1100
season pass

Segway Magical History Tours
magicalhistorytour.com
Minneapolis: 125 Main St SE
952.888.9200
13+ years

Viewing the Mississippi River from the Science Museum of Minnesota

American Wings Air Museum
www.americanwings.org
Blaine: 8891 Airport Rd
763.786.4146

Choo Choo Bob's
choochoobobs.com/store
St. Paul: 2050 Marshall Ave
651.646.5252, parties, story time
Chinook C281, 10/31/15
Chinook mobile 8/31/15

EAA Young Eagles
tinyurl.com/mok3yj
Blaine: *tinyurl.com/pmebtwy*
Lake Elmo: *tinyurl.com/kmwo9v2*
So St. Paul: *tinyurl.com/mtexl3j*
Lakeville: *tinyurl.com/mazjkol*
Red Wing: *tinyurl.com/mbbu9dc*
White Bear Lake: *745.eaachapter.org*
free airplane rides 8—17 years

Excelsior Streetcar Line
tinyurl.com/l3vjtcp
952.922.1096

Friends of the 261
261.com
Shoreview: 4322 Lakepoint Ct

Hennepin Overland Railway
hennepinoverland.org
Minneapolis: 2501 38th St E
612.276.9034

Minnesota Air National Guard Museum
mnangmuseum.org
St. Paul: 670 General Miller Dr, Bldg 670
612.713.2523, parties

Minnesota Transportation Museum
mtmuseum.org
St. Paul: 193 Pennsylvania Ave E
651.228.0263
tots and trains, *tinyurl.com/nf7exju*,
MPR

Jackson Street Roundhouse Osceola and St. Croix Valley Railway
Osceola: 114 Depot Rd
715.755.3570

Minnesota Streetcar Museum
trolleyride.org
Minneapolis: 4200 Queen Ave S
952.992.1096
camps, events
tinyurl.com/m869k38

Minnehaha Depot
tinyurl.com/lgbyckr
Minneapolis: Hwy 55 &
Minnehaha Parkway
651.228.0263

The Museum of Lake Minnetonka
steamboatminnehaha.org
Excelsior: 37 Water St
952.474.2115
Wayzata: 402 E Lake St
952.474.2115

The Museum of Lake Minnetonka
steamboatminnehaha.org
Excelsior: 37 Water St
Wayzata: 402 E Lake St
952.474.2115

Twin City Model Railroad Museum
tcmrm.org
St. Paul: 1021 Bandana Blvd E
651.647.9628, parties

World War II Aviation Museum
cafmn.org
So St. Paul: 310 Airport Rd
Hanger #3, Fleming Field

Spring (March—May)

Art-A-Whirl—*nemaa.org/art-a-whirl*

Cinco de Mayo
cincodemayosaintpaul.com/parade.html

Earth Day—*tinyurl.com/q3mjygl*

Festival of Nations—*festivalofnations.com*

Flint Hills International Children's Fest
ordway.org/festival/

Irish Fair—*irishfair.com*

Irish Festival—*irishfair.com*

Lakewood Cemetery Memorial Day
lakewoodcemetery.com/memorial_day.html

Mayday Parade and Festival—*hobt.org/mayday/*

Minnesota Horse Expo—*mnhorseexpo.org*

Northwest Sportshow—*northwestsportshow.com*

Omnifest—*smm.org/omnifest*

Rock the Cradle—*tinyurl.com/mqr3euz*

Saint Patrick's Day Parade—*stpatsassoc.org*

Saint Paul Art Crawl—*stpaulartcrawl.org*

Shepherd's Harvest Sheep and Wool Festival
www.shepherdsharvestfestival.org

Shrine Circus—*osmancircus.com*

Wishes for the Sky—*wishesforthesky.org*

Summer (June—August)

Aquatennial—*tinyurl.com/mfl9njv*

Commemorative Air Force Hanger Dance
tinyurl.com/qyg4nbr

Discover Aviation Hanger Dance
tinyurl.com/lgxuwho

Edina Art Fair—*edinaartfair.com*

Grand Old Day—*grandave.com*

Highland Fest—*highlandfest.com*

Highland Park Water Tower—*tinyurl.com/m7ajtc9*

Midsommar Dag—*tinyurl.com/pegsmgt*

Paws on Grand—*grandave.com/events/paws-grand*

Saint Anthony Park Arts Festival
stanthonyparkartsfestival.org

St. Patrick's Day of Irish Dance—*tinyurl.com/mqjggnz*

Selby Ave Jazz Festival—*selbyavejazzfest.com*

Twin Cities Jazz Festival—*hotsummerjazz.com*

Fall (August—November)

Grand Harvest—*grandave.com/events*

Dia de Los Muertos—*tinyurl.com/nfxvlpp*

Fall into the Arts Festival—*tinyurl.com/9nxgxjm*

Halloween Parades—*anokahalloween.com*

Highland Water Tower—*tinyurl.com/m7ajtc9*

Minnesota State Fair—*mnstatefair.org*

Monarch Festival—*monarchfestival.org*

Renaissance Festival—*renaissancefest.com*

Sever's Corn Maze—*severscornmaze.com*

Thrill Kenwood—*tinyurl.com/px7y2yw*

Trail of Terror—*trailofterrormn.com*

Twin Cities Harvest Festival
twincitiesmaze.com

Victorian Ghost Stories—*tinyurl.com/p75ov3d*

Woofstock—*dogsmn.com/woofstock.html*

Zurah Shrine Club Circus—*tinyurl.com/ppwcu46*

Winter (November—February)

A Christmas Carol—*guthrietheater.org*

Black History Events—*tinyurl.com/lo2px5v*

Film Society of Minneapolis/St. Paul
mspfilmsociety.org

Grand Meander—*grandave.com/events*

Holidazzle Village—*holidazzle.com*

Kwanzaa Family Celebration—*tinyurl.com/lxqwajw*

Loyce Houlton's Nutcracker—*mndance.org*

Minnesota Parent Camp Fair—*mnparent.com*

Reindeer Day —*tinyurl.com/mqz3jqk*

Rev. Martin Luther King, Jr Day Events
tinyurl.com/mkmpt8e

Santaland—*macys.com*

Santa Train—*tinyurl.com/mxd6gmt*

St. Paul Winter Carnival—*winter-carnival.com*

TwinsFest—*tinyurl.com/be5rxv*

Urban Expeditions—*tinyurl.com/n8jkv7w*

Schubert Family Concerts
schubert.org/musicinthepark/family

Shakespeare Classic, Guthrie Theater
guthrietheater.org/Shakespeare

Victorian Christmas—*tinyurl.com/l62plt4*

YMCA—*ymcatwincities.org*
Scholarships—*tinyurl.com/n84rjj8*
Andover: 15200 Hanson Blvd, 763.230.9622
Burnsville: 13850 Portland Ave, 952.898.9622
Coon Rapids: 8950 Springbrook Dr NW 763.785.7882
Eagan: 550 Opperman Dr, 651.456.9622
Edina: 7355 York Ave S, 952.835.2567
Elk River: 13337 Business Ctr Dr NW, 763.230.2800
Hastings: 85 Pleasant Dr, 651.480.8887
Hudson: 2211 Vine St, 715.386.1616
Lino Lakes: 7690 Village Dr, 651.795.9622
Minneapolis: 1015 4th Ave N, 612.821.2193
Minneapolis: 30 S 9th St, 612.371.9622
Minneapolis: 3335 Blaisdell Ave, 612.827.5401
Minneapolis: 1711 W Broadway Ave, 612.588.9484
Minneapolis: 30 S 9th St, 612.371.9622
Minneapolis: 1801 University Ave SE, 612.676.7700
Minnetonka: 12301 Ridgedale Dr, 952.544.7708
New Hope: 7601 42nd Ave N, 763.535.4800
Prior Lake: 3575 N Berens Rd NW, 952.230.9622
St. Paul: 875 Arcade St, 651.771.8881
St. Paul: 1761 University Ave W, 651.646.4557
St. Paul: 194 East 6th St, 651.292.4143
Shoreview: 3760 Lexington Ave N, 651.483.2671
West St. Paul: 150 Thompson Ave E, 651.457.0048
White Bear Lake: 2100 Orchard Ln, 651.777.8103
Woodbury: 2175 Radio Dr, 651.731.9507

YWCA, parties
ywcampls.org
Minneapolis: 2808 Hennepin Ave S, 612.874.7131
Minneapolis: 2121 East Lake St, 612.215.4333
Minneapolis: 1130 Nicollet Mall, 612.332.0501

ywcaofstpaul.org
St. Paul: 375 Selby Ave 651.222.3741

Boys & Girls Club—*boysandgirls.org*
Minneapolis: 2410 Irving Ave N, 612.522.3636
Minneapolis: 1607 51st Ave N, 612.668.1663
Minneapolis: 4320 Newton Ave N, 612.668.2015
Minneapolis: 701 E 39th St, 612.822.3191
Minneapolis: 2495 18th Ave S, 612.455.2818
St. Paul: 1620 Ames Ave, 651.774.5654
St. Paul: 690 Jackson St, 651.221.0330
St. Paul: 291 East Belvidere, 651.222.2212
Mound: 7000 Cty Rd 15, 952.472.4581

Boy Scouts Northern Star Council
northernstarbsa.org, 763.231.7201
St. Paul: 393 Marshall Ave
Golden Valley: 5300 Glenwood Ave

Girl Scouts River Valleys
www.girlscoutsrv.org, 800.845.0787
St. Paul: 400 Robert St S
Brooklyn Center: 5601 Brooklyn Blvd
Burnsville Satellite Shop: 1000 E 146th St, Ste 1149
Chanhassen Satellite Shop: 600 W 78th St, Ste 10D

Photo courtesy Amy Cook

Animal Humane Society
animalhumanesociety.org
Buffalo: 4375 Hwy 55 SE
763.390.3647
Coon Rapids: 1411 Main St NW
763.862.4030
Golden Valley: 845 Meadow Ln N
763.522.4325
St. Paul: 1115 Beulah Ln
651.645.7387
Woodbury: 9785 Hudson Rd
651.730.6008
camps, parties volunteering

Como Park Zoo
comozooconservatory.org
St. Paul: 1225 Eastabrook Dr
1100 Hamline Ave, 651.487.8200
Entertainment mobile & online,
TPT, 1-3 years free Thurs
tinyurl.com/n9rhd9z
camps, classes, parties

Department of Animal Science
tinyurl.com/lllnqbh
St. Paul: University of Minnesota
305 Haecker Hall, 1364 Eckles Ave
612.624.2722

Fur-Ever Wild
fureverwild.org
Lakeville: 10132 235th St W
612.467.9653, parties

Minnesota Zoo
mnzoo.org
Apple Valley: 13000 Zoo Blvd
952.431.9200, camps, parties
AAA, *bloomington-coupons.com*
Chinook C-190, 10/15/15
Chinook mobile 8/31/15

The Raptor Center
www.raptor.cvm.umn.edu
St. Paul: 1920 Fitch Ave
612.624.4745, parties

Reptile and Amphibian
Discovery Zoo
theradzoo.com
Entertainment D46, 10/31/15
Owatonna: 3297 Cty Rd 45 N
888.472.3966

Sea Life Minnesota Aquarium
visitsealife.com/Minnesota
Bloomington: Mall of America
952.883.0202, memberships
parties, AAA, *tinyurl.com/o5wmt7v*
bloomington-coupons.com 12/31/15
Chinook C191, 10/31/15
Chinook mobile 8/31/15
Entertainment D11—13, 94, 12/30/15
Entertainment mobile & online
MOA 52—55, 237-238, 12/31/15, TPT

Secondhand Hounds
secondhandhounds.org
Minnetonka: 4340 Shady Oak Rd
952.322.7643, parties

Wildlife Science Center
wildlifesciencecenter.org
Columbus: 5463 Broadway Ave W
651.464.3993

Sea life at the Minnesota Zoo

Index

Index

Index

Index

40295898R00040

Made in the USA
Lexington, KY
31 March 2015